Lecture Notes in Computer Science   11300

Commenced Publication in 1973
Founding and Former Series Editors:
Gerhard Goos, Juris Hartmanis, and Jan van Leeuwen

More information about this series at http://www.springer.com/series/7409

Pierluigi Contucci · Andrea Omicini
Danilo Pianini · Alina Sîrbu (Eds.)

The Future
of Digital Democracy

An Interdisciplinary Approach

 Springer

Editors
Pierluigi Contucci ⓘ
University of Bologna
Bologna, Italy

Danilo Pianini ⓘ
University of Bologna
Cesena, Italy

Andrea Omicini ⓘ
University of Bologna
Cesena, Italy

Alina Sîrbu ⓘ
University of Pisa
Pisa, Italy

ISSN 0302-9743 ISSN 1611-3349 (electronic)
Lecture Notes in Computer Science
ISBN 978-3-030-05332-1 ISBN 978-3-030-05333-8 (eBook)
https://doi.org/10.1007/978-3-030-05333-8

Library of Congress Control Number: 2018963118

LNCS Sublibrary: SL3 – Information Systems and Applications, incl. Internet/Web, and HCI

This Springer imprint is published by the registered company Springer Nature Switzerland AG
The registered company address is: Gewerbestrasse 11, 6330 Cham, Switzerland

Preface

One of the most widespread misconceptions about the form of government that we call *democracy* is the *one man one vote* synthesis. In fact, this appears nowhere in the document most commonly considered the democracy manifesto, the speech by Pericles to the Athenians, as reported by Thucydides. From there, as well as from other beginnings, democracy has evolved following different historical tortuous paths, in a complex process of accumulation that has created institutions, laws, professions, and – unfortunately – misconceptions.

Tipping points along those paths have mainly occurred when structural revolutions have happened. The supply of energy, for instance, has been accompanied by radical changes in societal organization, and its daily consumption per capita rose from the 2,000 calories of our prehistory to the current 100,000 of the Western world, with a major sudden jump around the industrial revolution. In a similar way, the daily consumption of information per capita, albeit more difficult to measure, has grown enormously in the same time interval, due to the so-called digital revolution. The purpose of this volume is to analyze changes induced by this digital revolution in the Western political system and whether these changes are more (or less!) aligned with democratic principles.

But: *What is democracy?* The concept of democracy is one of the most complex and articulated in human culture. While it is based on suggestive ideas like the participation of all people to political and civic life and the protection of human rights, it also acts mostly with an oversimplified voting instrument like the majority rule on a single choice. It is no surprise, therefore, that its realization faces issues at many levels— especially with representing minorities and dealing with participation of people without a basic education. The question is, can we address some of those issues by changing the instruments used, by employing novel ideas in the field of social choice theory, and – possibly – through the *digital revolution?*

A paramount fact that has been observed in the past few decades is that political engagement is decreasing, especially in younger citizens, and when it is present it assumes a totally different shape. This can be due to several factors, including disappointment in election results, mistrust in society and politicians, lack of belief in the political system itself or in every one's power to make a difference. At the same time, participation in democratic life follows rules and usages that have emerged in the past couple of centuries, in times when *communication* was mostly different from today. *Horizontal communication* followed a slow, short-range, peer to peer path, while *vertical communication* was fast from institutions to citizens through traditional media.

Nowadays, instead, communication is much faster, and flows in every direction. Since communication is the basal fabric on which society is defined, it appears obvious that the civic organization and politics itself should adapt to the new status. Institutional inertia, nevertheless, causes large delays in updating and adapting. Therefore, the balance between *participation* and *delegated representation* that worked relatively well after the Second World War is now facing a crisis.

A thorough understanding of the factors involved in participation is a first step toward providing solutions. Using the Internet to fill the gap and build a digital democracy provides an opportunity, along with several risks that need to be carefully analyzed. In order for this volume to achieve its objectives, it needs to be implemented using a fully inter- and trans-disciplinary perspective. This includes the social sciences, traditionally concerned with these topics, but, importantly, also the hard sciences, in particular mathematics and computer science, which provide a critical contribution to the field. The volume is thus organized in six chapters.

The first contribution ("Young People as Engaged Citizens: A Difficult Challenge Between Disillusionments and Hopes"), by Bruna Zani and Elvira Cicognani, precisely addresses the problem of disengagement of young people from political participation. By providing a fresh look on the sociological research on the subject, the authors discuss the causes of the disinterest from the classic forms participation, as well as the new forms of engagement, along with the factors that separate young people involved in new patterns of engagement and actions of participation from the inactive ones. Clearly, the focus here is on the new forms of participation and engagement, in particular on those based on the digital platforms, and on how these new forms may help and encourage youngsters to participate, express themselves, and possibly have their voice heard at national and European levels.

Yet, whereas sociological and politic aspects are essential to understand the current state of democracy and possibly foresee its future, there are technical aspects that have to be explored—even before digital ones. This is why the the second contribution ("Experiments on the Reaction of Citizens to New Voting Rules: A Survey," by Jean-François Laslier) deals with *voting* itself, by discussing experiments and tests—lab, on-line, and in-situ voting experiments. In accordance with the overall scope of the book, the author focuses on the effect of *innovation* in politics—and in voting, in particular: how it affects the perception of the voters, their understanding, and their behavior, as well as how it does change the overall results of the voting.

The mathematics of voting is the theme of the third contribution ("Egalitarianism vs. Utilitarianism in Preferential Voting," by Pierluigi Contucci and Alina Sîrbu). In particular, the authors introduce a novel mathematical approach to shape the new forms of democratic participation that involves social choice theory. Most (political) elections today require voters to select one option out of many, and results are based on majority votes. However, this oversimplifies voter opinions, limiting the individual freedom of expression, leaving instead ample maneuver room to the preliminary phases of the voting process. Additionally, due to the loss of information, results of the votes often do not correspond to the actual position of the population. This results in generating frustration and disappointment, and causing citizens to ignore subsequent elections. However, various other means to organize an election exist. For instance, ballots can be *rankings* of candidates, or *ratings*, with algorithms to extract the winner that can be fairer. Although significant research on these alternative voting systems has been performed (starting as early as the 18th century by Condorcet), they remain mostly unused. This is because no consensus exists on which method is best, while some methods can be also computationally expensive. Thus, the authors analyze preferential voting, where voters are required to rank candidates. After reviewing the classic Condorcet criterium introduced to maximize the total satisfaction of voters, i.e., the utilitarian criterion, the authors describe a method to minimize the total un-evenness of the rewards, i.e., the egalitarian dimension. It is shown, through various examples, that the egalitarian dimension can produce fairer results, and also provide resilience to radicalism.

The fourth contribution ("Knowledge Management for Democratic Governance of Socio-Technical Systems," by Jeremy Pitt, Ada Diaconescu, and Josiah Ober) relates the notion of *self-governing socio-technical system* (as well as self-governed institutions) to the success of Athenian democracy. The authors focus on the critical issue of *knowledge management* (knowledge aggregation, alignment, codification), and point out a number of emerging technologies that could work as the building blocks for democratic self-governance in socio-technical systems. After the discussion of the many open issues, the need for *responsible design* is emphasized, along with technologies promoting continuous re-design and self-organization—since "democracy is not an end state."

The fifth contribution ("The Problematic Relationship Between Trust and Democracy; Its Crisis and Web Dangers and Promises," by Cristiano Castelfranchi and Rino Falcone) discusses the articulated relationship between on-line and representative democracy. The authors claim first of all that digital democracy should not replace, but rather integrate representative democracy by leveraging computational tools and platforms. Then, they elaborate on the notion of (bilateral) trust in the relationship between people and their representatives (and institutions), arguing that even in the digital era trust remains an absolutely crucial issue to democracy.

Whereas sociological, political, psychologic, mathematical, and computational aspects are indeed essential to digital democracy, engineering issues are not to be overlooked whenever *digital platforms* become one of the main stages for the political play. Thus, the sixth (and final) contribution ("Democratic Process and Digital Platforms: An Engineering Perspective," by Danilo Pianini and Andrea Omicini) elaborate on the huge (and often hidden) impact that digital technologies (potentially) have over all key processes in human societies—including the democratic one. The authors review the main tools and platforms for digital democracy, and point out how their tumultuous emergence in the past decade have left a number of essential concerns unanswered: in particular, the issue of the engineering process. By looking at the most common platforms for digital democracy, the authors show how the lack of care (and correct practice) in the software engineering of the digital platform invariably leads to critical problems for digital democracy. The most critical issues are pointed out, along with their potential (negative) impact on the democratic process.

Overall, the construction of this volume took several months—many more than expected, indeed. Other contributions were not included, not because of their lack in quality, but mainly because (in accordance with authors) we found them not precisely placed where this book was meant to be. The editors of this volume would then like to thank all the contributors – those who appear and also those who do not – for the many discussions we had with them, which really helped to shape the book in its final form.

Digital democracy is a hot topic nowadays, and is going to become hotter, its relevance growing along with the impact of computational platforms on our (political) life. We are truly confident that this volume will contribute to a better understanding of the potential and dangers of digital democracy, possibly helping readers by going beyond the misunderstandings, the misconceptions, and the conceptual and practical abuses that the very notion of democracy is undergoing during this age of technological revolution and social turmoils.

June 2018   Pierluigi Contucci
                                                                   Andrea Omicini
                                                                   Danilo Pianini
                                                                   Alina Sîrbu

Organization

"The Future of Democracy" was an ISA Topic 2016 event, sponsored by the Istituto di Studi Avanzati (ISA, Institute of Advanced Studies) of the Alma Mater Studiorum— Università di Bologna. It was organized in the context of the project "Il futuro della partecipazione democratica dei cittadini" (The Future of Citizens' Democratic Participation), by Pierluigi Contucci, Marco Albertini, Giampiero Giacomello, Pina Lalli, Elvira Cicognani, and Andrea Omicini—all from Bologna's Alma Mater.

The event was held in the Aula dei Poeti, at the Università di Bologna, on November 3, 2016, and articulated in two half-day meetings: a scientific workshop and a dissemination panel.

Scientific Workshop "The Future of Democracy"

The first one (the scientific workshop "The Future of Democracy") was devoted to the scientific discussion of all of the many facets of the issue of digital democracy. Held in the morning, it focused on the multi- and inter-disciplinary issues that affect digital democracy—mathematical, computational, political, economical, sociological, and political issues. After the presentation, the discussion was really lively, and produced many of the seeds that led to the elaboration of the present volume.

Speakers

Virginia Dignum	TU Delft, The Netherlands
Giampiero Giacomello	Università di Bologna, Italy
Dirk Helbing	ETH Zurich, Switzerland
Jean-François Laslier	Paris School of Economics and CNRS, France
Andreas Nitsche	Association for Interactive Democracy, Berlin, Germany
Danilo Pianini	Università di Bologna, Italy
Alina Sîrbu	Università di Pisa, Italy
Bruna Zani	Università di Bologna, Italy

Dissemination Panel "Il futuro della democrazia"

The second one (the panel "Il futuro della democrazia") involved representatives from the institutions, the culture, and the citizens, and was devoted to extend the perception of the main perspective and issues of digital democracy beyond the walls of academia.

Panelists

Chiara Alvisi	Università di Bologna, Italy
Massimo Fustini	Regione Emilia-Romagna, Italy
Daniela Giannetti	Università di Bologna, Italy

Matteo Lepore	Comune di Bologna, Italy
Terri Mannarini	Università del Salento, Italy
Marco Roccetti	Università di Bologna, Italy

Sponsoring Institutions

Finally, the event was sponsored by the following institutions:

- Institute of Advanced Studies (ISA)
  http://www.isa.unibo.it
- ALMA MATER STUDIORUM—Università di Bologna, Italy
  http://unibo.it
- Dipartimento di Matematica (DM), Università di Bologna, Italy
  http://mathematics.unibo.it
- Dipartimento di Informatica – Scienza e Ingegneria (DISI), Università di Bologna, Italy
  http://informatics.unibo.it
- Dipartimento di Scienze Politiche e Sociali (DSPS), Università di Bologna, Italy
  http://dsps.unibo.it

Contents

Young People as Engaged Citizens: A Difficult Challenge Between
Disillusionments and Hopes 1
    Bruna Zani and Elvira Cicognani

Experiments on the Reaction of Citizens to New Voting Rules: A Survey . . . 14
    Jean-François Laslier

Egalitarianism vs. Utilitarianism in Preferential Voting. 24
    Pierluigi Contucci and Alina Sîrbu

Knowledge Management for Democratic Governance
of Socio-Technical Systems 38
    Jeremy Pitt, Ada Diaconescu, and Josiah Ober

The Problematic Relationship Between Trust and Democracy; Its Crisis
and Web Dangers and Promises 62
    Cristiano Castelfranchi and Rino Falcone

Democratic Process and Digital Platforms: An Engineering Perspective 83
    Danilo Pianini and Andrea Omicini

Author Index 97

Subject Index 99

Young People as Engaged Citizens: A Difficult Challenge Between Disillusionments and Hopes

Bruna Zani and Elvira Cicognani(✉)

Alma Mater Studiorum–Università di Bologna, Bologna, Italy
{bruna.zani,elvira.cicognani}@unibo.it

Abstract. The presence of young people as engaged active citizens in the political scenario seems to be declining in recent years all over Europe. However, whereas many young people are disinterested in politics and political participation, others are active political actors involved in new patterns of engagement and actions of participation. What are the factors leading some youth to be politically active and others not? There are multiple explanations for this phenomenon, and it is crucial for the future of citizens' democratic participation to understand the position that young people might take between apathy and participation. The present chapter aims to contribute to this focusing on the psychosocial factors and processes that facilitate and hinder youth's political and civic engagement with particular attention to the new forms of participation and engagement, including digital ones, that youngsters adopt to have their voice heard at national and European levels.

Keywords: Participation · Engagement · Citizenship · Adolescents · Young people

1 Introduction

The aim of this chapter is to contribute to the scientific debate on political and civic participation by focusing on the psychological factors and processes that have been identified as significant influences on participation in the empirical literature. In particular, we will focus on research studies that have examined participatory phenomena among youth, by drawing from contributions provided by two large cross national EU-funded projects, PIDOP [26] and CATCH-EyoU [9].

Researchers' interest toward young people engagement and participation has grown steadily in the last three decades, within different disciplines (e.g., political science, sociology, education, psychology, media studies). A central reason is the generalised decline, in different countries, of the degree of involvement – particularly of the younger generation – in traditional forms of political participation (e.g., membership and volunteering for political parties), as consistently shown by cross-national surveys throughout Europe and beyond. As a consequence, a social narrative has emerged – within policy and scientific discourses,

© Springer Nature Switzerland AG 2019
P. Contucci et al. (Eds.): *The Future of Digital Democracy*, LNCS 11300, pp. 1–13, 2019.
https://doi.org/10.1007/978-3-030-05333-8_1

as well as in the media – which describes young people as generally "uninterested", "unengaged" towards social and political issues in their communities and societies. Such condition would pose serious challenges for the future of our democracies, as far as it may be indicative of shortcomings in the political and civic socialization processes of the new generations.

However, as researchers have broadened their analysis of young people participation practices, a different picture has emerged, which shows that some young people are indeed involved in other less conventional forms of participation at civic level (e.g., volunteering, petitions, boycotting, etc.) as well as online [34]. Young people have often pronounced civic and political interests—particularly in issues at the local level (including issues of litter, graffiti, local transport, local amenities, etc.) as well as in broader environmental, humanitarian and human rights issues at the international or global levels. In addition, ethnic minority and migrant youth often have a high level of interest in issues affecting their own ethnic community and issues affecting their country of origin or the country of origin of their parents. However, young people tend to tackle these issues through civic and non-conventional forms of participation (e.g., charitable activities, consumer activism, demonstrations and petitions) rather than through conventional forms of participation (e.g., voting). Online forms of political participation (e.g., through SMS, blogs, etc.) are particularly widespread among youth and are considered powerful tools for moving young people into political participation, due also to their greater accessibility [39]. Therefore, they have attracted a growing research interest, in order to understand the factors that motivate young people to participate online vs. to engage into more conventional offline forms of civic and political action (e.g., [5,10]). An issue of debate is how online and offline modes of participation interact [39]: some authors argue that they work independently and represent distinct forms of engagement; others assume strong interrelations among them, by seeing them as alternative means for political action; and still others posit spill-over effects from online and offline participation, thus reinforcing and enlarging the potentials of one another. Empirical longitudinal evidence has indicated that for adolescents online activities act like a gateway for other offline political participation modes. For young adults, however, conventional political participation spills over into Internet activities [21].

These debates, and related research evidence suggest that, while traditional forms of political participation such as voting are currently in decline in many European countries, this trend may not be indicative of public disengagement per se but of a shift to a qualitatively different kind of public activism, based on the creative use of a range of different means and forms, including online modes. If this is the case, then the prognosis that the process of generational replacement will inevitably result, over time, in a significant erosion of the public engagement of citizens may well be wrong. In fact, research into civic socialization in young people has shown that adolescents' engagement within community and youth organisations predicts longitudinally political engagement and participation in later life [32,38] and promotes a sense of belonging to one's community as well as personal and social competencies for political action [2]. However, the processes which are currently driving younger people away from conventional political participation such as voting, towards other forms of participation are poorly understood.

Moreover, it became clear that, to better understand the nature of the emerging forms of youth participation and their meanings, multidisciplinary efforts were needed. Key research questions that have been addressed are the following:

- Why do many young citizens fail to vote in elections?
- Why are young people turning increasingly to street demonstrations, charitable activities, consumer activism and social media to express their political and civic views?
- What are the factors that lead some young people to engage in political and civic action?
- What are the barriers which hinder political participation by young people?
- How can greater levels of engagement with public issues be encouraged among all citizens and especially among youth?

There are multiple reasons and motivations for this phenomenon according to the theoretical perspectives adopted by researchers, and it is crucial for the future of citizens' democratic participation to understand the position that young people might take between apathy and participation.

2 Youth Political and Civic Engagement: Definitions and Forms of Participation

A common definition of *political participation* adopted by researchers within political and social sciences is

> activity that has the intent or effect of influencing either regional, national or supranational governance, either directly by affecting the making or implementation of public policy, or indirectly by influencing the selection of individuals who make that policy. [38]

Political participation is generally distinguished conceptually into *conventional forms of activity* involving electoral processes (e.g., voting, election campaigning, running for election, and more generally, volunteering for political partiers) and *non-conventional forms of activity* which occur outside electoral processes (e.g., signing petitions, participating in political demonstrations, displaying a symbol or sign representing support for a political cause, membership of political campaigning organizations, etc.) [6].

Political participation is considered distinct from *civic participation*, by which we mean *voluntary activity focused on helping others, achieving a public good, or participating in the life of a community, including work undertaken either alone or in cooperation with others in order to effect change*—see [6, 43]. Forms of civic engagement or participation include a variety of activities such as: working collectively to solve a community problem; belonging to community organizations;

attending meetings about issues of concern; raising money for charity; helping neighbours; consumer activism (boycotting and buycotting).

In the literature we can find other types of categorisations of forms of participation (e.g., manifest vs. latent). In the attempt to fully capture the variety of forms of participation, Ekman and Amnå [14] have developed a broader typology. The typology considers participation at both the *individual level and the collective level*; moreover, it discriminates between *latent and manifest forms* of political behaviour. Further, and interestingly, the typology also incorporates a *non-participation category*, in order to capture the full spectrum of participation and discriminate between *apolitical* (passive form) and *antipolitical* (active form) motives for lack of engagement.

Besides the forms and contexts in which engagement and participation occur, another issue of debate in this multidisciplinary literature is the degree of engagement that is expected from citizens in order to ensure a well-functioning representative democracy. On this point, Amnå and Ekman [4] have recently introduced the notion of *standby citizens* to explain the patterns of young people generalised political passivity evidenced by several research findings on conventional political participation (electoral). According to these authors, such a notion represents a political orientation that transcends the conventional active/passive dichotomy, suggesting a new way of analysing citizens' political *and non-participatory* behaviour. In a research on political socialisation of Swedish adolescents, four distinct groups were identified, characterised by different citizenship orientations: *active* youths (who score high on both measures of political interest and political participation); those on *standby* (scoring high on interest but only average on participation); the *unengaged* (scoring low on both interest and participation); and the *disillusioned* (scoring low on participation and lowest of all groups on interest). Interestingly, the 'standby' category is the largest group, suggesting that it represents a common orientation for young people in contemporary democracies.

On the other hand, the emerging research on online youth political participation suggests that social media use, through their mobilising potential, may initiate new patterns of political participation in the digital age [39].

3   Factors and Processes Influencing Civic and Political Participation

Research studies that have attempted to explain the different levels and forms of youth civic and political engagement have considered a range of interconnected factors, that can be summarised by locating them at different ecological levels; such factors intersect with individual psychological processes that contribute to explaining individual variability in participatory behaviours within the same groups and contexts. We can distinguish at least *four* different levels of factors: *macro-level contextual* factors, *proximal social* factors, *psychological* factors, and also *demographic* factors.

3.1 Demographic Factors

Civic and political participation appears to differ according to sociodemographic factors; among the most influential ones are individual's age, socioeconomic status, gender, ethnicity. Civic and political participation shows a tendency to increase from adolescence to young adulthood. There is good evidence that individuals of lower socioeconomic status (*SES*) often exhibit lower levels of political and civic engagement and participation: they tend to have poorer political and civic knowledge [30] and participate civically and politically to a lower extent [17,43]. For example, two of the main indices of SES, education and income, are both independently related to political knowledge [13]; to interest in politics and voting [8]; and to the likelihood of volunteering, attending community meetings and working on neighbourhood problems [17]. Education is the principal driver, influencing the civic skills that individuals exercise in their jobs and other organisations as well as their later social networks. These civic skills and social networks influence various aspects of psychological engagement (including political attentiveness, political interest and political knowledge) and various forms of political and civic participation (such as voting, protesting, working with others on community problems and attending meetings on a regular basis) [23,38].

Males and females often differ in their levels of political interest, participation in voluntary organisations and voter turnout. In particular, research findings indicate a higher involvement of men in political participation and of women in civic forms of participation; such differences seem to be present since adolescence [11]. Previous research has identified a wide range of factors that are responsible for gender differences in political participation [20]. These factors can be grouped into three broad categories: cultural and societal (e.g., the religion of a country, the level of economic development of a country, the longevity of democratic traditions within a country), social (e.g., level of education, labour force participation, marriage, motherhood) and civic (e.g., degree of participation in informal politics, membership of voluntary civic organisations) [18]. However, precisely how these various factors interact to generate the differences in patterns of participation between women and men is still not well understood. Among the obstacles that are reported as hindering women political participation there are gender stereotypes and limited resources for participation, due to traditional gender roles—see [11].

There are differences in political and civic engagement also as a function of *ethnicity,* even after income and educational attainment have been taken into account [17]. Ethnic minorities and migrants exhibit lower levels of political participation than members of national majority groups, a pattern which is not surprising given the restrictive criteria and practices and the racism and discrimination that often prevent minority and migrant individuals from getting fully involved in the political life of the country in which they live [1,33]. Such a finding has been found to be associated with a variety of factors. These include: cultural and societal factors (culture, political institutions and opportunities available within the country of residence, political regimes); demographic factors (migrant generational status, employment status, education); social factors (membership of civic organizations, social norms); and individual and psychological factors (fluency in the language of the country of residence, political values, knowledge of civic and political institutions in the country of residence, sense of belonging) [10]. However, there is currently a poor understanding of how these various factors interact to generate patterns of participation by minority and migrant individuals.

Most of these findings are based on research studies examining offline political and civic engagement. Emerging research on the role of social media use have stressed the equaliser qualities of these means of engagement, along the lines of socioeconomic status, gender and ethnicity [39], potentially contributing to reversing the pattern of inequality in youth participation.

3.2   Macro-level Contextual Factors

Macro-level contextual factors influencing civic and political participation include structural influences on individuals' participation, which have been investigated especially within political sciences, sociology, social policy (e.g., historical factors, cultural and religious differences, political ideologies, electoral systems, national policies). Relevant factors that have been found associated with political and civic participation are the following: degree of *fiscal, administrative and political decentralisation* of the state; procedures used by members of the political system to deal with challengers; *discursive opportunity structure* (prevailing discourse about acceptability and legitimacy of different forms of action); *rules and design of the electoral system*; *population* size, concentration, stability, homogeneity and cohesion; *rules for granting nationality and citizenship* to migrants; levels of *racism and discrimination* against minorities and migrants; availability of *organizational and community networks*; *historical longevity of democratic traditions* in a country; level of *economic development* of a country; *cultural and religious heritage* of the country and of the country of origin [6].

3.3   Proximal Social Factors

By *proximal factors* we mean the social contexts in which young people develop and their influences; e.g., family, educational context, community organisations, the media. Such factors have been investigated particularly from a psychosocial and sociological perspective. Relevant *family factors* that have an impact upon young people participation include, for example, parental socioeconomic status, parental education, parental ethnicity, parenting style, family communication style, political talk in the family home, parental political party preferences, having a daily newspaper and books in the home, parental civic volunteering. Research studies have found that young people participation is enhanced when there is an open communication in the family on political issues and when parents adopt an authoritative parenting, as well as by parents' positive norms about political and civic participation and parents' own engagement [11].*Peer group factors* include positive peer relationships, degree of peer group integration and solidarity, peers' political beliefs and behaviour. *Education factors* refer to the contents of the school curriculum (e.g., whether it promotes participation experiences), open and democratic classroom climate, opportunities offered by the school for participation in school or college councils, school-based community service. *Organizational membership factors* include quantity and quality of participatory experiences in extracurricular activities within community groups and organisations (e.g., volunteering, religious); for example, adolescents' membership in a range of organisation during adolescence positively predicts young people civic engagement, as well as future political participation [3]. Youth workers, youth and leisure centres, youth and education NGOs, and leaders of community organisations often play a crucial role in relationship to youth participation, especially in relationship to hard-to-reach and disengaged young people. The quality of participatory experiences (e.g., whether they stimulate reflection and critical awareness) is important in further encouraging involvement. *Workplace factors* include labour force participation, workplace experiences, trade union membership. *Religion* may impact on participation through religious affiliation, religiosity, membership of a place of worship, etc.

Among the proximal factors, a specific attention is needed for the role of the media context in youth participation. *Media factors* concern attending to news on the television and in newspapers, general levels of television watching, internet usage. Media are extremely important for young people, with TV, radio, the Internet and new social media (i.e., Facebook, Twitter and YouTube) being among the main sources from which youth obtain their information about civic and political issues and means for actual engagement [39]. It has been noticed that social media have several mobilising potentials making it easier for individuals to engage in online versions of several political actions, such as participating in political discussions, persuading others how to vote, as well as engaging in a variety of forms of online activism. Further, social media may foster informal discussions about politics, which have traditionally been associated with higher levels of political engagement—see also Subsect. 3.4. Some specific attributes of the SMS (e.g., news feeds) may increase young people accidental exposure to social and political contents (particularly during electoral campaigns), contributing to the formation of social norms and potentially enhancing their engagement.

3.4 Psychological Factors

There is a wide range of psychological factors that empirical research has found to be associated with political and civic participation. These factors include *cognitive factors* such as knowledge, beliefs, attitudes, opinions and social and cultural values, all of which have been found to be linked to patterns of participation and engagement—e.g. [43]. Three specific cognitions that have been found to significantly enhance young people political participation are political interest, political attentiveness, and internal efficacy [25, 41]. Research studies indicate that young people frequently feel that they do not know enough about political issues to be able to engage in effective action to influence political, civic and social change, and this lack of knowledge is experienced by them as a significant impediment to their own civic and political participation. More recently, Dahl *et al.* [12], in their analysis of a large sample of adolescents from different EU countries, found that young people political passivity is affected by feelings of *apathy* (lack of desire and motivation to take an interest in politics) and *alienation* (sense of estrangement from the politics and government and of powerlessness and normlessness). Alienated youth are more likely to seek more unconventional ways to influence public affairs.

Related to cognitive factors is *personality*: for example, Russo and Amnå [29] found, in a study on young adults, that online forms of political participation reflect partly different personality profiles (e.g., individuals open to experience and extraverts are more likely to engage online vs. other personality types).

Emotions also predict levels of civic and political participation and engagement. Usually, attention has been given to negative emotions as precursors of participation (e.g. anger, resentment, fear, dissatisfaction), associated with perceived injustice and relative personal and group deprivation. However, as the literature on volunteerism and community participation indicates, positive emotions (e.g., satisfaction, sense of purpose, feelings of emotional connection) might also be important to explain sustained engagement [22].

The role of *(social and collective) identity* is central and has been widely recognised in the literature on different forms of participation. Dominant theoretical perspectives are social identity theory (SIT) and its subsequent developments [36]. Social identification with one's group or community has a central role in the explanation of collective action and community participation. Specifically, adolescence is a crucial period for the formation of a mature adult identity, including civic and political identity, which entails young people negotiation of their role as political citizens. Associated with social identification *is sense of belonging*, capturing the emotional quality of the relationships with the group. Among both adults and young people, sense of community and social identification with the community have been found to be positively associated with civic and political participation [2].

Perceived control/efficacy, power and competences also play an important role. In the social movement studies, power is conceived in terms of a struggle between social groups and as a societal or intergroup issue. Power is also a personal and an interpersonal phenomenon: people decide to engage in participatory behaviours in the context of groups if they perceive that they can have an influence and be taken into consideration inside the groups. These processes have a central importance in motivating young people to participate: research evidence indicates that young people often feel that they are not taken seriously in political terms by politicians and other older adults—this lack of responsiveness reduces their belief in their own ability to have any influence politically or civically and is experienced as a significant disincentive to engage any further with political issues. Moreover, when young people engage in acts of political participation, they feel that adults fail to represent their participatory actions with fairness and seriousness of purpose.

Existing research has also revealed that social *trust*, political trust (i.e., in politicians, political institutions and the political system as a whole) and external *efficacy* (i.e., the belief that politicians and political institutions are responsive to citizens' views) are related to various aspects of participation and engagement [35, 37].

Traditional models of political participation have underscored the role of *motives and goals* for participation. The notion of *individual motives* has also been considered in the literature on volunteering (e.g. functional models of volunteering processes, according to which people volunteer to satisfy some individual needs) [24]. The role of motives and goals has also been emphasised in the collective action literature, where other possible motives for participation have been pointed out (e.g., expressing one's values, influencing public opinion, altruistic motives, etc.). The theoretical literature on collective action suggests the usefulness of distinguishing among different levels of goals: personal goals, collective goals and personal and social values. Moreover, besides these classifications, qualitative data collected on young people's perceived motives of different forms of participation (political, civic, non-conventional, school) confirmed that different types of motives are present [40].

Finally, people's perceptions of *opportunities for*, and *barriers* to, participation are also linked to their patterns of participation. Opportunities are provided by structures for participation such as associations and social networks, which need to be perceived as being open and accessible [16, 27], while people can perceive barriers for a number of reasons, including their own limited economic resources, lack of time and poor education [28, 38].

These various psychological factors have been investigated empirically as predictors of different forms of participation (e.g., political, volunteering, collective action, vote), including online forms of participation, and they appear to interact with one another in complex ways. Individual psychological factors sometimes moderate or amplify the effects of other factors (e.g., at macro-social or proximal level), and sometimes their effects on participation are mediated by other psychological factors rather than being direct [42]. In general, political attentiveness, political interest, internal efficacy, external efficacy, institutional trust, social trust, ideological identity are all significant predictors of both political and civic participation.

Emler [15], in his effort to create an integrative model of the influences on political participation, has identified a number of factors which determine individuals' capacity and inclination for participation: political interest, political attentiveness, political knowledge, political opinions, self-efficacy, ideological commitment and cost-benefit calculations. However, these psychological factors in turn are related to a host of *social factors*, including education, membership of organisations and associations (which provide contexts for political discussion and mobilisation), income, occupational prominence and social network centrality. In addition, Emler argues that these social factors, which of course all vary demographically, interact with aspects of the *macro-political context*, especially institutional design, with the decentralisation of institutional structures and the horizontal separation of powers being implicated here in particular: thus, in states in which institutions are characterised by greater decentralisation, organisational membership and political discussion are more strongly associated with political participation. Emler concludes that the decline in participation in recent years is probably due to the decline in personal ties at the social level which have resulted from recent changes in occupational and recreational patterns and lifestyle.

4 Conclusion

The previous review clearly shows how complex is the range of factors and processes that appear to play a role in the explanation of young people civic and political engagement. There are, however, some consistent findings across empirical studies that indicate that young people who are more active in their society and communities are generally more interested in social and political issues and perceive a stronger efficacy at personal level (e.g., feeling to be capable to engage in participatory behaviours and to make a difference) and collective level (e.g. as members of groups). Such feelings are strengthened by participatory experiences of "good quality", capable to facilitate learning processes, that youth can have opportunity to experience in school and within a variety of community organisations. These experiences also contribute to strengthening young people sense of belonging to the community and social wellbeing, which, in turn, are conducive to future engagement.

Most of the research reviewed in this chapter has investigated civic and political participation at local and national levels. Less attention has been devoted to understanding how young people understand the EU and their citizenship at EU level, and how they engage in European issues. Recent research within the CATCH-EyoU project [9] indicates that the two levels of citizenship (national and EU) should be distinguished as they have partly different predictors—e.g., [31]. This suggests that future research should distinguish young people according to different levels of belonging (local, national, EU, global) when investigating their civic and political engagement.

Considering the approaches to encourage young people to develop an interest in social and political issues and become politically active, the importance of engaging youth through the use of participatory approaches (e.g., Participatory Action Research with Youth or YPAR, Youth-Adult partnerships) has been pointed out—for example, through their active collaboration in the analysis of social issues and development of proposals of change. Moreover, the role of online technologies (including playful digital civic education and gamification, e.g., [7,19] in strengthening and sustaining young people political engagement (e.g., through the use of participatory platforms) is recently being investigated and tested by specific interventions. In view of the involvement of the younger generations with these technologies, one question that deserves greater attention at both theoretical and intervention level is whether these means may represent something more than an alternative instrument for participation, possibly creating a new kind of participatory citizenry.

References

1. Ahmad, N., Pinnock, K.: Civic participation: potential differences between ethnic groups. Research project, Commission for Racial Equality, London, UK (2007). http://luna.manchester.ac.uk/MediaManager/srvr?mediafile=/MISC/Manchester~23~23/5910/AIURRRC_000008.pdf
2. Albanesi, C., Cicognani, E., Zani, B.: Sense of community, civic engagement and social well-being in Italian adolescents. J. Community Appl. Soc. Psychol. **17**(5), 387–406 (2007). http://onlinelibrary.wiley.com/doi/10.1002/casp.903/full
3. Albanesi, C., Mazzoni, D., Cicognani, E., Zani, B.: Predictors of civic and political participation among native and migrant youth in Italy: the role of organizational membership, sense of community and perceived social well-being. In: Barrett, M., Zani, B. (eds.) [6], chap. 15, pp. 268–291. http://www.routledge.com/Political-and-Civic-Engagement-Multidiscip linary-perspectives/Barrett-Zani/p/book/9780415704687
4. Amnå, E., Ekman, J.: Standby citizens: understanding non-participation in contemporary democracies. In: Barrett, M., Zani, B. (eds.) [6], chap. 6, pp. 96–108. http://www.routledge.com/Political-and-Civic-Engagement-Multidisciplinary-perspectives/Barrett-Zani/p/book/9780415704687
5. Banaji, S., Buckingham, D.: The Civic Web: Young People, the Internet, and Civic Participation. MIT Press, Cambridge (2013). http://mitpress.mit.edu/books/civic-web
6. Barrett, M., Zani, B. (eds.): Political and Civic Engagement. Multidisciplinary Perspectives. Routledge, London (2015). http://www.routledge.com/Political-and-Civic-Engagement-Multidisciplinary-perspectives/Barrett-Zani/p/book/9780415704687
7. Barthel, M.L.: President for a day: video games as youth civic education. Inf. Commun. Soc. **16**(1), 28–42 (2013). https://doi.org/10.1080/1369118X.2011.627176
8. Bynner, J., Schuller, T., Fienstein, L.: Wider benefits of education: skills, higher education and civic engagement. Zeitschrift für Pädagogik **49**(3), 341–361 (2003). http://eric.ed.gov/?id=EJ676728
9. CATCH-EyoU: Constructing AcTive CitizensHip with European Youth: Policies, practices, challenges and solutions (2015–2018). http://cordis.europa.eu/project/rcn/194593_en.html
10. Cicognani, E., Albanesi, C., Mazzoni, D., Prati, G., Zani, B.: Explaining offline and online civic engagement intentions between Italian and migrant youth. Revista de Psicología Social **31**, 282–316 (2016). http://www.tandfonline.com/10.1080/02134748.2016.1143177
11. Cicognani, E., Zani, B., Fournier, B., Gavray, C., Born, M.: Gender differences in youths' political engagement and participation. Role of parents and of adolescents' social and civic participation. J. Adolesc. **35**(3), 561–576 (2012). https://doi.org/10.1016/j.adolescence.2011.10.002
12. Dahl, V., et al.: Apathy or alienation? Political passivity among youths across eight European Union countries. Eur. J. Dev. Psychol. **15**(3), 284–301 (2018). https://doi.org/10.1080/17405629.2017.1404985
13. Delli Carpini, M.X., Keeter, S.: What Americans Know About Politics and Why it Matters. Yale University Press, New Haven (1996). http://yalebooks.yale.edu/book/9780300062564/what-americans-know-about-politics-and-why-it-matters
14. Ekman, J., Amnå, E.: Political participation and civic engagement: towards a new typology. Hum. Aff. **22**(3), 283–300 (2012). http://www.degruyter.com/view/j/humaff.2012.22.issue-3/s13374-012-0024-1/s13374-012-0024-1.xml

15. Emler, N.P.: Explaining political participation: integrating levels of analysis. In: Barrett, M., Zani, B. (eds.) [6], chap. 9, pp. 146–161. http://www.routledge.com/ Political-and-Civic-Engagement-Multidisciplinary-perspectives/Barrett-Zani/p/ book/9780415704687

16. Evans, S.D.: Youth sense of community: voice and power in community contexts. J. Community Psychol. **35**(6), 693–709 (2007). https://doi.org/10.1002/jcop.20173

17. Foster-Bey, J.: Do race, ethnicity, citizenship and socio-economic status determine civic engagement? CIRCLE Working Paper 62, Center for Information and Research on Civic Learning and Engagement (CIRCLE), December 2008. http:// files.eric.ed.gov/fulltext/ED505266.pdf

18. Galligan, Y.: Influencing women's civic and political participation: contextual and individual determinants. In: Barrett, M., Zani, B. (eds.) [6], chap. 3, pp. 54–70. http://www.routledge.com/Political-and-Civic-Engagement-Multidisciplinary-per spectives/Barrett-Zani/p/book/9780415704687

19. Hassan, L.: Governments should play games: towards a framework for the gamification of civic engagement platforms. Simul. Gaming **48**(2), 249–267 (2017). https:// doi.org/10.1177/1046878116683581

20. Inglehart, R., Norris, P.: Rising Tide: Gender Equality and Culture Change Around the World. Cambridge University Press, Cambridge (2003). http://www. cambridge.org/us/academic/subjects/politics-international-relations/politics-gen eral-interest/rising-tide-gender-equality-and-cultural-change-around-world

21. Kim, Y., Russo, S., Amnå, E.: The longitudinal relation between online and offline political participation among youth at two different developmental stages. New Media Soc. **19**(6), 899–917 (2017). https://doi.org/10.1177/1461444815624181

22. Leach, C.W., Iyer, A., Pedersen, A.: Anger and guilt about in group advantage explain the willingness for political action. Pers. Soc. Psychol. Bull. **32**(9), 1232–1245 (2006). https://doi.org/10.1177/0146167206289729

23. Nie, N.H., Junn, J., Stehlik-Barry, K.: Education and Democratic Citizenship in America. The University of Chicago Press, Chicago (1996). http://press.uchicago. edu/ucp/books/book/chicago/E/bo3683564.html

24. Omoto, A.M., Snyder, M.: Considerations of community: the context and process of volunteerism. Am. Behav. Sci. **45**(5), 846–867 (2002). https://doi.org/10.1177/ 0002764202045005007

25. Pasek, J., Feldman, L., Romer, D., Jamieson, K.H.: Schools as incubators of democratic participation: building long-term political efficacy with civic education. Appl. Dev. Sci. **12**(1), 26–37 (2008). https://doi.org/10.1080/10888690801910526

26. PIDOP: Processes Influencing Democratic Ownership and Participation (2009–2012). http://cordis.europa.eu/project/rcn/91492_en.html

27. Putnam, R.D.: Bowling Alone: The Collapse and Revival of American Community. Simon & Schuster, New York (2000). http://www.simonandschuster.com/books/ Bowling-Alone/Robert-D-Putnam/9780743203043

28. Rosenstone, S.J., Hansen, J.M., Reeves, K.: Mobilization, Participation, and Democracy in America. MacMillan, New York (1993). http://www.pearson.com/ us/higher-education/program/Rosenstone-Mobilization-Participation-and-Democr acy-in-America-Longman-Classics-Edition/PGM169000.html

29. Russo, S., Amnå, E.: The personality divide: do personality traits differentially predict online political engagement? Soc. Sci. Comput. Rev. **34**(3), 259–277 (2016). https://doi.org/10.1177/0894439315582487

30. Schulz, W., Ainley, J., Fraillon, J., Kerr, D., Losito, B.: Initial Findings from the IEA International Civic and Citizenship Education Study. International Association for the Evaluation of Educational Achievement (IEA), Amsterdam (2010). http://research.acer.edu.au/civics/5/

31. Šerek, J., Jugert, P.: Young European citizens: an individual by context perspective on adolescent European citizenship. Eur. J. Dev. Psychol. **15**(3), 302–323 (2018). https://doi.org/10.1080/17405629.2017.1366308

32. Sherrod, L.R., Flanagan, C., Youniss, J.: Dimensions of citizenship and opportunities for youth development: the what, why, when, where, and who of citizenship development. Appl. Dev. Sci. **6**(4), 264–272 (2002). https://doi.org/10.1207/s1532480xads0604_14

33. Sherrod, L.R., Torney-Purta, J., Flanagan, C.A.: The civic life of Latina/o immigrant youth: challenging boundaries and creating safe spaces. In: Handbook of Research on Civic Engagement in Youth [34], chap. 17, pp. 445–470. http://onlinelibrary.wiley.com/doi/10.1002/9780470767603.ch17

34. Sherrod, L.R., Torney-Purta, J., Flanagan, C.A. (eds.): Handbook of Research on Civic Engagement in Youth. Wiley, Hoboken (2010). https://doi.org/10.1002/9780470767603

35. Stolle, D.: Social capital. In: Dalton, R.J., Klingemann, H. (eds.) The Oxford Handbook of Political Behavior. Oxford University Press, Oxford (2007). http://www.oxfordhandbooks.com/view/10.1093/oxfordhb/9780199270125.001.0001/oxfordhb-9780199270125-e-035

36. Tajfel, H., Turner, J.C.: The social identity theory of intergroup behavior. In: Worchel, S., Austin, W.G. (ed.) Psychology of Intergroup Relations, chap. 1, pp. 7–24. Nelson-Hall Publishers, Chicago (1986)

37. Torney-Purta, J., Henry Barber, C., Richardson, W.K.: Trust in government-related institutions and political engagement among adolescents in six countries. Acta Politica **39**(4), 380–406 (2004). https://doi.org/10.1057/palgrave.ap.5500080

38. Verba, S., Schlozman, K.L., Brady, H.: Voice and Equality: Civic Voluntarism in American Politics. Harvard University Press, Cambridge (1995). http://www.hup.harvard.edu/catalog.php?isbn=9780674942936

39. Xenos, M., Vromen, A., Loader, B.D.: The great equalizer? Patterns of social media use and youth political engagement in three advanced democracies. Inf. Commun. Soc. **17**(2: The Networked Young Citizen), 151–167 (2014). https://doi.org/10.1080/1369118X.2013.871318

40. Zani, B., Cicognani, E., Albanesi, C.: La partecipazione civica e politica deigiovani. Discorsi, esperienze, significati. Heuresis. Scienze sociali, CLUEB, Bologna (2011)

41. van Zomeren, M., Postmes, T., Spears, R.: Toward an integrative social identity model of collective action: a quantitative research synthesis of three socio-psychological perspectives. Psychol. Bull. **134**(4), 504–535 (2008). http://psycnet.apa.org/record/2008-08177-005

42. van Zomeren, M., Spears, R., Fischer, A.H., Leach, C.W.: Put your money where your mouth is! Explaining collective action tendencies through group-base danger and group efficacy. J. Pers. Soc. Psychol. **87**(5), 649–664 (2004). https://doi.org/10.1037/0022-3514.87.5.649

43. Zukin, C., Keeter, S., Andolina, M., Jenkins, K., Delli Carpini, M.X.: A New Engagement? Political Participation, Civic Life, and the Changing American Citizen. Oxford University Press, Oxford (2006). http://global.oup.com/academic/product/a-new-engagement-9780195183160

Experiments on the Reaction of Citizens to New Voting Rules: A Survey

Jean-François Laslier[✉][iD]

CNRS, Paris School of Economics, 48 Boulevard Jourdan, 75014 Paris, France
`jean-francois.laslier@ens.fr`

Abstract. This paper is a survey of what we learned from experiments about how innovations in the field of voting are received. Different experimental methods have been used: in the laboratory, on line and in situ. Preferences for voting rules are driven by self-interest, by a quest for simplicity and are also correlated with political attitudes. For most rules, voters show no cognitive barriers to their use, but for more complex rules, serious misunderstanding can appear.

Keywords: Voting rules · On-line experiments · In-situ experiments

1 Introduction

Political theory, Social Choice theory as well as Game theory can hardly predict individual votes under different voting rules [2,15,37]. Various kinds of experiments, in the lab and on the field, were therefore designed to observe voters' behaviour. This was an occasion to see the cognitive processes at work in the understanding—or misunderstanding—of voting processes, and to see how people react when offered to participate to "scientific" experiments about institutional and democratic questions. These observations make possible the study of some questions relevant for the design of institutions: Are people willing to engage in experiments in Politics? What kind of people like what kind of innovation in this field? What are the cognitive, psychological or social barriers to innovation?

Different experimental methodologies are used in Political Science [12,22, 26], each of which has advantages and disadvantages. *(i)* In the tradition of Experimental Economics , work can be done in the laboratory, controlling voters' preferences through monetary payoffs. *(ii)* Closer to the tradition of Political Science, work can be done in surveys, and in particular in on-line surveys. *(iii)* In a more original fashion, work can be done *in situ*, that is, in the time and place of a real election.

Note that work done in Political Psychology usually takes as fixed the political preferences of the subjects but manipulates the information provided to them—see for instance Kleiberg and Lau [27]. This stream of research will not be surveyed here, despite the obvious relevance of the problems of information

© Springer Nature Switzerland AG 2019
P. Contucci et al. (Eds.): *The Future of Digital Democracy*, LNCS 11300, pp. 14–23, 2019.
https://doi.org/10.1007/978-3-030-05333-8_2

on political campaigning, because the discipline of Political Psychology has not been (for the moment and to my knowledge) essentially concerned by the question of institutional innovation, that is the central issue of this survey.

Most of the work done deals with a specific problem: single-winner elections of the "presidential" type, that is voting for choosing one out of a fixed list of alternatives, or choosing one candidate out of several. This specific problem is conceptually very simple and can be considered as an archetype of the collective decision question. Of course numerous other institutional arrangements exist that might and should be studied from the same point of view: parliamentary representation, balance of powers, public management and delegation, etc. But single-winner elections appear as the typical instance of the pure collective choice problem: there are several possibilities, we have to chose but we do not agree, how shall we proceed?

2   A Laboratory Experiment

This section describes an experiment in the sense of "Experimental Economics" [16]. Participants are recruited on a voluntary basis, they come to the lab to earn money without a priori knowing what the experiment is about, and play some kind of game that is proposed to them. The payment a participant earns at the end of the session is always positive but depends on what she has done, what the others have done, and maybe also on chance, in a manner that is clearly explained. The payment may differ from one participant to the other and it is made at the end of the session, in privacy.

The experiment presented in the remainder of this section is one of a number of similar investigations [18,19] and is described in depth in [41]. The game is an election, the rules of which are clearly explained, as follows.

There are 21 subjects, who will elect one among five alternative candidates, labeled A, B, C, D and E, symmetrically located at five distinct points on a horizontal axis, as in Fig. 1. There is an extreme left candidate (A, in position 1), a moderate left candidate (B, in position 6), a centrist candidate (C, in position 10), a moderate right candidate (D, in position 14), and an extreme right candidate (E, in position 19).

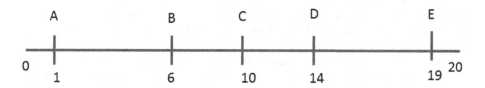

Fig. 1. Candidate positions

Each subject is located in one of the 21 points on the same horizontal axis (from 0 to 20). Positions are randomly assigned to participants, but in a way that all positions are filled. All this is known to the participants.

The payoff only depends on the elected candidate and the subject's position, according to the intuition: the closer the better. Subjects are informed that they will be paid 20 Euros minus the distance between the elected candidate's position and their own positions.

It is not clear, in such a situation, what to do as a voter. In order to let the possibility of individual learning and collective evolution, sequences of several elections are performed, with exactly the same protocol, and the same assignment of positions, the scores of the candidates being given after each. Which one of these elections is used to compute the payments is chosen randomly at the end of the session.

This is essentially the protocol. The treatment variable is the voting rule. During one session several sequences of elections are done, using different voting rules. Because this kind of elections are, throughout the world, almost always done using one-round or two-round majority voting, these voting rules are of particular interest, but scholars have also studied with this protocol more exotic rules such as Approval Voting, the Hare system of Single Transferable Vote, or the Borda rule.

Here I concentrate on three rules:

- First Past the Post (1R). Also known as "Plurality", or "One-round majority voting". Each voter gives the name of one candidate, the candidate with the largest number of votes is elected, and ties are broken randomly.[1]
- Two-Round majority voting (2R). A first vote takes place, like under Plurality. If a candidate gathers more than half of the votes, she is elected; otherwise the two candidates with the largest number of votes qualify for a second round. At the second round plurality is used.[2]
- Approval Voting (AV). Each voter approves, or not, independently, each candidate. The candidate approved by the largest number of voters is elected [14].[3]

What follows describes data collected on a total of 734 participants—for more details, see [9,10,41,42]. Table 1 shows how many of the elections were won by the various candidates. One can see to what extent the voting rule matters: Whatever the rule, the extremist candidates (A and E) are never elected. In 1R and 2R elections, candidate C (the centrist candidate, a *Condorcet winner* in our case) is elected in about half of the elections. Things are quite different under Approval Voting. In AV elections, C is almost always elected (79% of the elections).

A more detailed analysis of how individual votes change as the sequence of elections unfolds makes these observations understandable. As time goes, votes gather on two (for 1R elections) or three (for 2R elections) candidates. The three viable candidates are always the same for 2R elections (candidates B, C, D), but for 1R elections the pair of viable candidates is not the same in all elections (the

---

[1] 1R is mainly used in the Anglo-saxon tradition (India, USA, UK).

[2] For presidential-like elections, most countries use 2R, with variants.

[3] This rule is not used for political presidential-like elections.

Table 1. Winning candidates (208 elections)

	1R	2R	AV
C	49%	54%	79%
B or D	51%	45%	21%
A or E	0	0	0
Total	92	92	24

pair of viable candidates is always composed of two candidates among the set B, C, D). On the contrary, votes under AV do not show time-dependence effects.

One can observe in the lab several features developed by the theory of voting. With the same preference profile, voting rules tend to elect the Condorcet winner (Approval Voting), or designate a candidate which depends on history (1R and 2R).

The fact that the result of the popular vote depends on history the way it does in these experiments is a nice example of *path-dependency*. It is a consequence of the voters not wanting to waste their single votes in systems (1R or 2R) in which they have to vote for one and only one candidate. This "desertion of the non-viable candidates" [15] opens the possibility of self-confirming predictions and information bubbles. From the game-theoretical point of view (which is a priori very relevant here since the participants are paid according to the result of the game), the possibility of path-dependency relates to the multiplicity of equilibria. Voting games often admit plenty of Nash equilibria. For instance, under First Past the Post any vote result in which the winning candidate is two or more votes ahead of the second-ranked one, is supported by a Nash equilibrium. And refinements of the Nash concept [35,36] generally face the same problem: strategic voting is really a coordination problem. The phenomenon is not seen with Approval Voting, simply because, under this rule, the voter can vote for as many candidates she wants.

This kind of laboratory experiments shows that different voting rules can lead to different results, that voters learn from the past, and that some rules are prone to path-dependency effects. This observation confirms what the rational theory of voting has already noticed, but other theoretical predictions are dis-confirmed in the laboratory. Rationality under two-round majority voting sometimes requires strategies that are more subtle that desertion of non-viable candidates. This more sophisticated behaviour is hardly seen in the lab [40].

One can argue that laboratory experiments in the Economics tradition are intrinsically biased in the direction of rational behaviour: subjects are paid for acting rationally, so it is no surprise that they do so, but it does not mean that the same will occur outside the lab, in real elections. There may be a trade-off between the possibility offered in the lab to control many parameters, in particular to control preferences through the use of monetary payments, and external validity [23,38]. It is therefore important to see to what extent the findings of the laboratory can be observed in less fabricated settings.

3   *In-Situ* Experiments

Starting in 2002 [3, 32, 33] several experiments have been performed using an original *in-situ* protocol. The experiments are performed on the day of an important political election (for instance the French presidential election) and in the place where people vote for real. After they voted officially, voters are invited to proceed to a second, un-official, vote, using a different voting rule.

Participation is free, but de facto restricted to people who voted in the real election (among other things, this precludes duplicate votes). We respect the decorum of the true election, in particular anonymity: participants fill their experimental ballot behind a curtain and put it in a closed urn.

Information has been provided before the election day. Whenever possible, all registered voters in the district where the experiment is done receive a letter at their personal address, that explains that this experiment is done for scientific reasons, and that explains precisely the voting rule. In Africa, in the weeks before the election day, assistants go to visit people to explain verbally what is going to be done [25]. Town meetings can also be organised for the same purpose, and the whole operation requires the active cooperation of the local authorities.

Most of these experiments has dealt with various forms of evaluative voting. Under evaluative voting, the voter freely grades each candidate on a fixed numerical scale, and the winner is the candidate who gets the largest total. Approval Voting can be seen as the simplest form of evaluative voting, where the scale is just $\{0, 1\}$. The other scales that are commonly tested are $\{0, 1, 2\}$, $\{-1, 0, 1\}$, and $\{0, 1, 2, 3, \ldots, 20\}$.

Because we know (from laboratory experiments as well as from classical political science research) that, in reality, voters think ahead before deciding who to vote for, it is important to distinguish these voting experiments from surveys that ask voters to rank or to evaluate the candidates. A key point is that participants have a correct idea of how ballots are counted. Laslier (2011) [28] discusses this point and related ones: understanding how to fill the ballot, understanding how ballots are counted and understanding what are the possible consequences of using one voting rule or the other. He argues that the logic of evaluative voting, that is to weight more or less in favour of one candidate or the other, in an additive way, matches the intuition of voters, so that additive evaluative rules do not generate serious misunderstanding, even for those participants who have only listened with one ear to the provided explanations.

A remarkable feature of these experiments is the high participation rate. People obviously appreciate that scientists take the time to ask for their participation, they understand that it can be useful, and most of them agree to spend time for the experiment. The participation rates are usually larger than 50%. The largest rate was obtained in the village of Gy-les-Nonains, France, in 2002. Out of 482 registered voters[4] there, 395 came to vote this day, and had the opportunity to participate to the experiment, turning the experiment

---

[4] That is almost the whole population over 18. In France almost all citizens are registered, even if they do not vote.

into a kind of social event. (On social pressure and turnout, see [20]) Out of these 395 persons, 365, that is 92.4%, participated. Participation is lower if the experiment is more time-demanding. Recent experiments ask voters to vote several times, using different rules, and ask them to fill a small socio-economic and political questionnaire. Typical figures for the participation rate are reported by Igersheim et al. [24]: 78% in 2002, 62% in 2007, 54% in 2012.

By design, these surveys do not select the participants. From the votes, one observes an important participation bias: more conservative voters participate less. This fact is interesting by itself, but it makes the analysis of the results of such experiments seriously more complicated.[5] The main result of this line of research is that evaluative, compared to single-name rules such as 1R and 2R, favours *Consensual candidates*. In Politics, these candidates are usually centrist candidates, who can gather support from moderate voters on both sides [1,6].

With respect to evaluative procedures, it is not clear to what extent the act of evaluating the candidates can replace the act of voting for one person [34]. Efforts have been made to distinguish between the various forms of evaluative voting and to understand more precisely how voters use grades: do scales matter? what is the specific importance of negative grades? are finer scales useful? It easy to see that scales do matter because the possibility of negative grades is detrimental to extremists candidates [4,6], but other conclusions must be considered as provisional.

The reader interested in knowing more about these experiences can refer to the survey by Baujard and Igersheim [5] or to the book by Dolez et al. [17].

4   On-Line Experiments

The *in-situ* protocol limits the amount of information one can gather from each individual observations, because it cannot be requested that the participants spend too much time inside the voting stations. It is thus impossible to have long questionnaires and to correlates many variables in the analysis. For this reasons, since Blais et al. [8] and Van der Straeten et al. [39], several scholars turned to on-line experimentation.

A web-site is created, that explains the voting rules of interest; participation is free and open, and the visitors are invited to vote in the current election according to the different rules. After they voted, they are invited to answer further questions. These sites thus fulfil two goals: public information (education or popular science) and research. For instance, the site that opened during the 2012 French presidential election [39] received several thousands of visitors, of which more than 8,000 made the whole exercise of reading, voting under three rules, and filling the questionnaire.

---

[5] Such a bias is intuitively understandable: by definition, conservative voters are less attracted by the idea of changing things, and our research is presented to the participants as: "Help us to study alternative voting rules." But still, one would like to deepen this point, that we observed repeatedly and that was, to the best of my knowledge, not previously noticed in the literature.

By checking IP adresses we can see that duplicate votes are almost inexistent in these surveys. But it is easy to see that, like the other methods previously described, the on-line method generates important participation bias: conservative voters tend to participate less. But the on-line questionnaires include socio-demographic, political and sociological questions that allow to correct the participation bias as well as sample selection would do, at least if the number of participants is large enough.

These experiments confirm the important finding that additive evaluative voting favor consensual candidates, that is, usually, centrist ones. Is this a good thing?

Blais et al. [11] studied the voters' preferences for voting rules, using data from the 2012 French presidential experiment [39]. They consider three reasons that might explain why a voter likes, or dislikes, a voting rule. The first one is *instrumental interest*: I like this rule, because it makes my favorite candidate win. The second motive is *expression*. The voting rules used in this experiment differ with respect to the expressive possibilities for the voter. Single-name balloting are the poorest, Approval Voting allows the expression of binary opinions about all candidates, and the Alternative Vote requires the voter to rank all the candidates, thus allowing a quite detailed expression. The third reason is *ideology*: besides the two first motives, one cannot exclude that people leaning to the left or to the right held different view on what is a "good" voting rule.

The authors in [11] find, with no surprise, that the two first reasons above are important, but the interesting point is that the third, ideological, motive is important too; namely, conservative voters tend to prefer rules like first-past-the-post where "voting" is just giving one name.

Leaving the world of presidential-like elections, Laslier et al. [30] studied the elections of the members of the European Parliament in 2014. The voting rules for the members of European Parliament vary from one country to another, in a number of dimensions, even if they are all of the "proportional" type. Most countries use party-list systems, and of particular interest is the fact that these party-list systems are more or less open.

Some countries (France, Spain) use *Closed party lists*: the voter just vote for one party and has no say about the candidates inside the list: candidates from each list are elected following the order on the list, which was decided ex ante. Latvia has a typical open-list system: each voter choses one and only one party, and gives points to the candidates on the list The elected candidates are picked from the list according to the support they personally received from the voters. Luxembourg has an even more flexible rule: it allows *Panachage* (voting for candidates of different lists) and *Cumulative voting* (giving two points to a candidate). These three systems are the ones used in the study [30], that was made throughout Europe and gathered 3672 respondents.

In all countries, the EuroVotePlus website was proposing to vote, under the three systems above, in a simulated election of 20 pan-European delegates, that is 20 members of the Parliament elected from euro-wide party lists, instead of being elected locally, as are actually all MEPs. On top of that, in some countries, the website was also proposing to use the three rules for the election of the respondents' local candidates.

The idea of electing some MEPs from a euro-wide constituency is an original proposal, that recently gained some support after the Brexit. The EuroVotePlus experiment allowed to check the acceptance of the pan-European district in the population.

It is found in [7, 13] that, in that setting, co-nationality remains a strong determinant of the votes: people tend to look for lists that contain more candidates of their nationality. Using the same data, Bettarelli et al. [7] and Golder et al. [21] show that open-list systems are more favourable to female representation, mainly because female respondents target female candidates.

5   Conclusion

All these experiments tend to show that electoral reforms are not particularly difficult, because people quickly master various election rules. Single-name balloting, according to which the voter is only required and allowed to provide the name of one candidate (or option) has several feasible alternatives which are not only supported by experts – see [29] – but also by the general population.

References

1. Alós-Ferrer, C., Granić, D.G.: Approval voting in Germany: description of a field experiment. In: Laslier and Sanver [31], pp. 397–411. https://doi.org/10.1007/978-3-642-02839-7_16
2. Austen-Smith, D., Banks, J.S.: Positive Political Theory I: Collective Preferenes. Michigan Studies in Political Analysis. University of Michigan Press (1999). http://www.press.umich.edu/14223
3. Balinski, M., Laraki, R., Laslier, J.F., Van der Straeten, K.: Le vote par assentiment: une expérience. Cahier du Laboratoire d'Econométrie del'Ecole Polytechnique 2003-013, Centre National de la Recherche Scientifique, Ecole Polytechnique (2003). http://hal.archives-ouvertes.fr/hal-00242959
4. Baujard, A., Gavrel, F., Igersheim, H., Laslier, J.F., Lebon, I.: How voters use grades in evaluative voting. European Journal of Political Economy (In press, available online). http://www.sciencedirect.com/science/article/pii/S0176268017300216, published on line 30 September 2017
5. Baujard, A., Igersheim, H.: Framed field experiments on approval voting: lessons from the 2002 and 2007 French presidential elections. In: Laslier and Sanver [31], pp. 357–396. https://doi.org/10.1007/978-3-642-02839-7_15
6. Baujard, A., Igersheim, H., Lebon, I., Gavrel, F., Laslier, J.F.: Who is favored by evaluative voting: an experiment conducted during the 2012 French presidential election. Elect. Stud. **34**, 131–145 (2014). http://www.sciencedirect.com/science/article/pii/S0261379413001807
7. Bettarelli, L., Iannantuoni, G., Manzoni, E., Rossi, F.: Voters' preferences and electoral systems. the EuroVotePlus experiment in Italy. Economia Politica **34**(1), 159–177 (2017). https://doi.org/10.1007/s40888-016-0046-y

8. Blais, A., Héroux-Legault, M., Stephenson, L., Gidengil, E.: Assessing the psychological and mechanical effect of electoral rules: a quasi-experiment. Elect. Stud. **31**(4), 829–837 (2012). http://www.sciencedirect.com/science/article/pii/S0261379412000753
9. Blais, A., Labbé-Saint Vincent, S., Laslier, J.F., Sauger, N., Van derStraeten, K.: Strategic vote choice in one-round and two-round elections: an experimental study. Polit. Res. Q. **64**(2), 637–645 (2011). https://doi.org/10.1177/1065912909358583
10. Blais, A., Laslier, J.F., Laurent, A., Sauger, N., Van der Straeten, K.: One round versus two round elections: an experimental study. Fr. Polit. **5**(3), 278–286 (2007). https://doi.org/10.1057/palgrave.fp.8200125
11. Blais, A., Laslier, J.F., Poinas, F., Van der Straeten, K.: Citizens' preferences about voting rules: self-interest, ideology, and sincerity. Public Choice **164**(3–4), 423–442 (2015). https://doi.org/10.1007/s11127-015-0287-2
12. Blais, A., Laslier, J.F., Van der Straeten, K. (eds.): Voting Experiments. Springer, Heidelberg (2016). https://doi.org/10.1007/978-3-319-40573-5
13. Bol, D., et al.: Addressing Europe's democratic deficit: an experimental evaluation of the pan-European district proposal. Eur. Union Polit. **17**(4), 525–545 (2016). https://doi.org/10.1177/1465116516630151
14. Brams, S.J., Fishburn, P.C.: Approval Voting. Birkhäuser, March 1983. http://www.springer.com/it/book/9780387498959
15. Cox, G.W.: Making votes count: strategic coordination in the world's electoral systems. Polit. Sci. Q. **113**(4), 724–725 (1998). https://doi.org/10.2307/2658266
16. Davis, D.D., Holt, C.A.: Experimental Economics. Princeton University Press, Princeton (1993). http://press.princeton.edu/titles/5255.html
17. Dolez, B., Grofman, B., Laurent, A. (eds.): In Situ and Laboratory Experiments on Electoral Law Reform: French Presidential Elections. Springer, New York (2011). https://doi.org/10.1007/978-1-4419-7539-3
18. Forsythe, R., Myerson, R.B., Rietz, T.A., Weber, R.J.: An experimenton coordination in multi-candidate elections: the importance of polls and election histories. Soc. Choice Welf. **10**(3), 223–247 (1993). https://doi.org/10.1007/BF00182507
19. Forsythe, R., Rietz, T.A., Myerson, R., Weber, R.J.: An experimental study of voting rules and polls in three-way elections. Int. J. Game Theory **25**(3), 355–383 (1996). https://doi.org/10.1007/BF02425262
20. Gerber, A.S., Green, D.P., Larimer, C.W.: Social pressure and voter turnout: evidence from a large scale field experiment. Am. Polit. Sci. Rev. **102**(1), 33–48 (2008). https://doi.org/10.1017/S000305540808009X
21. Golder, S.N., et al.: Votes for women: electoral systems and support for female candidates. Polit. Gend. **13**(1), 107–131 (2017). https://doi.org/10.1017/S1743923X16000684
22. Green, D.P., Gerber, A.S.: Reclaiming the experimental tradition in political science. In: Katznelson, I., Milner, H.V. (eds.) Political Science: State of the Discipline, Centennial edn, pp. 805–832. W. W. Norton, New York (2002)
23. Igersheim, H., Baujard, A., Gavrel, F., Laslier, J.-F., Lebon, I.: Individual Behavior under evaluative voting: a comparison between laboratory and *in situ* experiments. In: Blais et al. [12], pp. 257–269. https://doi.org/10.1007/978-3-319-40573-5_13
24. Igersheim, H., Baujard, A., Laslier, J.F.: La question du vote:expérimentation en laboratoire et in situ. L'Actualité Économique **92**(1–2), 151–189 (2016). http://econpapers.repec.org/article/risactuec/0140.htm
25. Kabre, P.A., Laslier, J.F., Van der Straeten, K., Wantchekon, L.: About political polarization in Africa: an experiment on approval voting in Benin (2013). http://pseweb.eu/ydepot/semin/texte1314/LAS2013ABO.pdf

26. Kittel, B., Luhan, W., Morton, R. (eds.): Experimental Political Science: Principles and Practices. Palgrave Macmillan, Basingstoke (2012). http://www.palgrave.com/gp/book/9780230300859
27. Kleinberg, M.S., Lau, R.R.: Candidate extremity, information environments, and affective polarization: three experiments using dynamic process tracing. In: Blais et al. [12], pp. 67–87. https://doi.org/10.1007/978-3-319-40573-5_4
28. Laslier, J.F.: Lessons from in situ experiments during French elections. In: Dolez et al. [17], pp. 91–104. https://doi.org/10.1007/978-1-4419-7539-3_5
29. Laslier, J.F.: And the loser is... plurality voting. In: Felsenthal, D.S., Machover, M. (eds.) Electoral Systems. Studies in Choice and Welfare, pp. 327–351. Springer, Heidelberg (2012). https://doi.org/10.1007/978-3-642-20441-8_13
30. Laslier, J.F., et al.: The EuroVotePlus experiment. Eur. Union Polit. **16**(4), 601–615 (2015). https://doi.org/10.1177/1465116515580180
31. Laslier, J.F., Sanver, M.R. (eds.): Handbook on Approval Voting. Studies in Choice and Welfare. Springer (2010). https://doi.org/10.1007/978-3-642-02839-7
32. Laslier, J.F., Van der Straeten, K.: Une expérience de vote par assentiment pendant la présidentielle de 2002: Analyse d'une expérience. Revue française de science politique **54**(1), 99–130 (2004). http://www.jstor.org/stable/43120029
33. Laslier, J.F., Van der Straeten, K.: A live experiment on approval voting. Exp. Econ. **11**(1), 97–105 (2008). https://doi.org/10.1007/s10683-006-9149-6
34. Lebon, I., Baujard, A., Gavrel, F., Igersheim, H., Laslier, J.F.: Opinions, strategic intentions and vote: a laboratory experiment using alternative proportional systems. In: Stephenson, L.B., Aldrich, J.H., Blais, A. (eds.) The Many Faces of Strategic Voting. Tactical Behavior in Electoral Systems Around the World. University of Michigan Press (2018, in press). http://www.press.umich.edu/9946174/many_faces_of_strategic_voting
35. Myerson, R.: Large Poisson games. J. Econ. Theory **94**(1), 7–45 (2000). http://www.sciencedirect.com/science/article/pii/S002205319892453X
36. Myerson, R., Weber, R.: A theory of voting equilibria. Am. Polit. Sci. Rev. **87**(1), 102–114 (1993). https://doi.org/10.2307/2938959
37. Ordeshook, P.C.: Game Theory and Political Theory: An Introduction. Cambridge University Press, Cambridge (1986). http://www.cambridge.org/us/academic/subjects/politics-international-relations/political-theory/game-theory-and-political-theory-introduction
38. Sauger, N., Blais, A., Laslier, J.F., Van der Straeten, K.: Strategic voting in the laboratory. In: Kittel et al. [26], pp. 95–111. http://www.palgrave.com/gp/book/9780230300859
39. Van der Straeten, K., Laslier, J.F., Blais, A.: Vote au pluriel: how people vote when offered to vote under different rules. PS: Polit. Sci. Polit. **46**(2), 324–328 (2013). https://doi.org/10.1017/S1049096513000036
40. Van der Straeten, K., Laslier, J.-F., Blais, A.: Patterns of strategic voting in run-off elections. In: Blais et al. [12], pp. 215–236. https://doi.org/10.1007/978-3-319-40573-5_11
41. Van der Straeten, K., Laslier, J.F., Sauger, N., Blais, A.: Strategic, sincere and heuristic voting under four election rules: an experimental study. Soc. Choice Welf. **35**(3), 435–472 (2010). https://doi.org/10.1007/s00355-010-0448-7
42. Van der Straeten, K., Sauger, N., Laslier, J.F., Blais, A.: Sorting out mechanical and psychological effects in candidate elections: an appraisal with experimental data. Br. J. Polit. Sci. **43**(4), 937–944 (2013). https://doi.org/10.1017/S0007123412000579

Egalitarianism vs. Utilitarianism in Preferential Voting

Pierluigi Contucci[1]([⊠]) [iD] and Alina Sîrbu[2] [iD]

[1] Department of Mathematics, Alma Mater Studiorum–Università di Bologna,
Bologna, Italy
pierluigi.contucci@unibo.it
[2] Department of Computer Science, Università di Pisa, Pisa, Italy
alina.sirbu@unipi.it

Abstract. Democratic societies base much of their decisions on voting procedures that involve aggregation of individual votes into a winning solution. While for two candidates majority voting can provide satisfactory results, for three or more candidates the winner depends on the voting method employed. In this chapter we analyse *preferential voting*, where voting ballots consist of a *ranking* of candidates. We first study the classical Condorcet criterium introduced to maximise the total satisfaction of voters, i.e. the *utilitarian criterion*. We then complement it with a recently introduced method to minimise the total un-evenness of the rewards, i.e. the *egalitarian dimension*. We show, through targeted examples and analysis of synthetic vote data, that the new dimension may lead to more fair results, and can provide resilience to radical voter opinions.

Keywords: Utilitarianism · Egalitarianism · Voting method
Opinion aggregation · Preferential voting · Condorcet paradox

1 Condorcet Theory of Democratic Vote

During the French Revolution and especially in the years before, due to the progressive delegitimisation of the King's political power, several intellectuals were advancing proposals to rationalise the steps taken by a group during deliberation. Among them a crucial topic of discussion was the selection of a solution among many alternatives, based on the opinion of the group members. This problem nowadays carries the name of *aggregation* of opinions or votes.

The mathematician Condorcet, in his treaty about the progress of the human spirit [2], in what he calls the tenth epoch, i.e. the future, foresees and hopes for an evolution of the social sciences in the same direction as the hard sciences at his times. He considers exemplary the degree of precision and trustability obtained through the systematic use of mathematics, and he claims that the same method should be applied to the organisation of society. Among the mathematical areas that are more suitable to achieve such results, probability must surely occupy a

© Springer Nature Switzerland AG 2019
P. Contucci et al. (Eds.): *The Future of Digital Democracy*, LNCS 11300, pp. 24–37, 2019.
https://doi.org/10.1007/978-3-030-05333-8_3

prominent place. In the same treaty he explains why, by giving several examples related to the rules to be applied in law and political debates.

In this introductory section we explain the main points of his theory of democratic vote and aggregation of opinions. Such ideas are today still at the foundation of the political sciences. Furthermore, with the enormous development of the internet, they are also used within branch of computer science concerned with sorting objects by relevance, with many applications in indexing and search.

The first paramount observation by Condorcet is the acknowledgment of the high level of complexity of the vote theory from its individual starting point up to the necessary synthesis to create consensus. In particular, he observes that the dichotomous option (yes or no, in favour or against, raised/unraised hands) is a funnel too narrow to express an individual opinion. It turns out to be a dramatic limitation of free expression and also easily manipulable in the preliminary stages of the vote. The starting point must therefore include at least a set of choices, options or candidates, that each individual can rank according to their preference. For example, in the case of a set of four candidates A, B, C, D, a vote is a ranking of the candidates, possibly with ties, of the form $A > D = C > B$, or, $D > C > A > B$, or $C = D > A > B$ etc.

This extension of the *space of expression* of the individual vote from dichotomous to multivalued has a precise meaning in mathematics: the local field of Condorcet voting theory takes values on the permutation group, or, if ties are allowed, on the Fubini group. Let us introduce some required notation. We will call v_i the vote of i-th voter of a group of N individuals. In general v_i will be a weak ordering of k candidates, i.e. an element of the set R_k, the Fubini group. The Fubini numbers are the cardinalities of those sets: $|R_1| = 1$, $|R_2| = 3$, $|R_3| = 13$, $|R_4| = 75$, $|R_5| = 541$ etc. With combinatorial-algebraic techniques one can show that $|R_k|$ grows slightly faster than an exponential, precisely by a multiplicative power-law factor c^k with $c \approx 1.44$. This information about the growth rate is more than a mere technicality. It tells us that if the number of candidates is of the order of the hundreds, like for instance for the problem of ranking the hotels of a middle-sized town, the space R_k is not inspectionable. That means that no computer either present or future can span it all since the time needed is well beyond the estimated age of the universe. Problems of this type are called NP-complete [9].

The way Condorcet proposes to *aggregate* the opinions reflects the political ideas of his times. We will exemplify with a concrete example: a high school having to decide where to go on a school trip. If the options are only two, say between Rome and Milan, the decision will turn out to be quite straightforward: by raising hands, the most voted option, the majority vote, is the only one compatible with the democratic principles. But if the options are three or more, hence when the topic has some complexity, new and unexpected effects may appear. Let us say that a class of sixty students must decide if going to London, Paris or Rome. The votes cast are represented in the following table:

30	20	10
Paris	Rome	London
Rome	Paris	Paris
London	London	Rome

which is: 30 students have voted the preference Paris > Rome > London, 20 students voted Rome > Paris > London and 10 London > Paris > Rome. We can then compare the options pairwise, i.e. by computing the number of students who prefer one city over another. We obtain:

- Paris wins over Rome 40 to 20
- Rome wins over London 50 to 10
- Paris wins over London 50 to 10

As a final result, the winning ranking is therefore: Paris > Rome > London.
Let us consider another example:

25	9	12	14
Paris	London	Rome	London
Rome	Paris	London	Rome
London	Rome	Paris	Paris

In this case pairwise comparison results in:

- Paris wins over Rome 34 to 26
- Rome wins over London 37 to 23
- London wins over Paris 35 to 25

This, clearly, does not admit any winner because a cycle appears in the preferences: Paris > Rome > London > Paris. This is known as the *Condorcet paradox*.

Condorcet proposes a solution to this problem, based on the notion of *distance* among votes defined as

$$d(v_1, v_2) = \text{minimum number of permutations to transform } v_1 \text{ into } v_2$$

A few examples of distances are:

- $d(A > B > C, B > A > C) = 1$ (swap A with B in the first ranking to obtain the second ranking)
- $d(A > B > C, C > A > B) = 2$ (swap B with C and then A with C)
- $d(A > B > C, C > B > A) = 3$ (swap A with B then A with C then B with C)

Using this measure, we can compute a distance between the result of an election and the vote cast by a voter. If we consider a winning ranking c the i-th voter is distant $d(v_i, c)$ from it. This quantity represents a measure of how unsatisfied with the outcome of the election the voter is. If we apply this to all voters, the total normalised distance from c (the mean distance) is:

$$\mu(c) = \frac{1}{N} \sum_{i=1}^{N} d(v_i, c).$$

This gives a measure of how unsatisfied all voters are, on average, with result c.

In order to choose a winner after a vote, we need to choose one suitable c. Condorcet proposes to select as a winner the solution c^* that minimises the mean distance from the electorate, μ. Such a choice corresponds to choosing the most satisfactory solution and, mathematically, is it obtained with the variational problem:

$$\inf_c \frac{1}{N} \sum_{i=1}^{N} d(v_i, c),$$

If we consider the second example previously discussed, we can take all possible rankings of the three candidate cities (6 possibilities), and compute for each of them the mean distance from all 60 students. This gives us a mean level of dissatisfaction for each possible outcome, and can be represented by the graph:

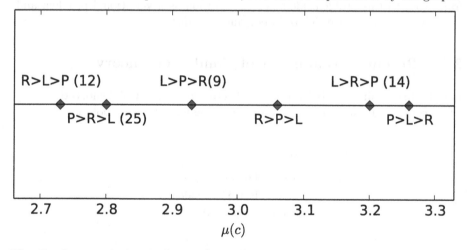

The Condorcet solution is that with smallest μ: hence, in this case, the solution is Rome > London > Paris.

The Condorcet solution, which can be non-unique, is the *median* of all the points with respect to the introduced distance, and not the *barycentre* among them. This distinction had already been clarified by Torricelli and Cavalieri: the median minimises the sum of the distances whereas the barycentre minimises the sum of the square distances. In spite of the that, the confusion of the two concepts keeps coming back, and sometimes causes harm. In 1919 the United States

Census Bureau defined the *population center* of a region using the barycentre instead of the median resulting in an incorrect computation. The mistake was corrected only ten years later by Corrado Gini in [5].

A few final remarks to conclude the section. It was discovered in 2001 that the medieval philosopher Ramon Lull knew already the combinatorial structure of the voting space and also the Condorcet solution [8]. The two contribution are in any case regarded as independent. In Lull's theory, probabilistic concepts are completely absent.

The distance introduced by Condorcet is only one possible way to make the Fubini space a metric space. Nowadays we know that those different metrics are classified in equivalence classes and have different impacts on different application fields. It is interesting to note that most of the research in this field are carried inside the tech giant companies like Yahoo, Google, and Facebook.

The theory introduced by Condorcet was later refined mathematically [7,11]. The distance between two votes is also known as the Kemeny distance, while the voting method can be found under the "Kemeny-Young" name as well.

Finally, we would like to note that although the nature of the notions introduced so far is combinatorial (the space of votes), geometric (the distance among votes), and analytical (the computation of minima), it is indeed the probabilistic nature that is most intrinsically linked to the problem we study: the v_i are, in modern terms, *random variables* describing the macroscopic behaviour of a system composed of N parts (the voters). Condorcet provides a mathematical framework to this problem identifying a solution as a variational problem and opens a new perspective rich of important consequences.

2   A Recent Development of Condorcet Theory

In order to explain a newly introduced idea toward a theory of democratic voting let us consider a different set of votes, this time with a strong polarisation:

101	99	1
Paris	London	Rome
Rome	Rome	London
London	Paris	Paris

Hence, 101 students prefer Paris > Rome > London, 99 students have the totally-opposite preference, London > Rome > Paris, and one other student prefers London > Rome > Paris. Condorcet theory would only allow to chose from the mean variational principle according to the evaluations of the mean distance (unsatisfaction):

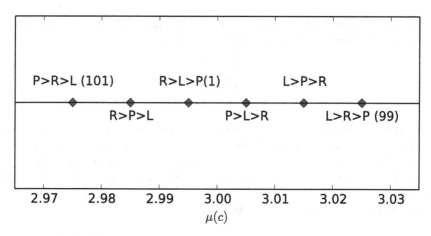

As expected, the Condorcet solution turns out to be $P > R > L$. However, please note the value of μ for the other possible rankings. The median solution is picking up a winning ranking according to the infinitesimal difference of three parts out of a thousand with respect to the second one $R > P > L$. Is this a good choice?

In order to better understand the question, let us go back to the choice among only two alternatives, when we use the majority rule to choose the winner. We know that large majority decisions are appreciated and have a strong stability in time. Instead, when the majority rule selects the result by small percentages, there is instability and turmoil. Is there a quantity that can measure this type of tension and instability?

Two examples might clarify the question. Let us consider the vote of 100 individuals choosing among two representatives, A and B. If A receives 95 votes and B 5 the obvious election of A makes 95 people happy and 5 unhappy. Calling $p = 0.95$ the average satisfaction is $2p-1 = 0.9$, which is the mean of the binomial distribution. In the case instead in which the two candidates get 51 and 49 votes, the Condorcet solution provides a mean satisfaction of about 0.02. Probability theory provides another important measure, the standard deviation $\sqrt{p(1-p)}$ which quantifies how unevenly is the satisfaction distributed among voters. The lower the standard deviation, the more even is the distribution of satisfaction. The computation of the standard deviation gives, in the first case, about 0.21, while in the second case it is 0.49, a value close to the maximum possible.

It is clear that the standard deviation has a high relevance in many questions of social choice theory because it averages the comparisons among individuals. In economic theory, where social choice is studied, it is well known that personal satisfaction is not only related to personal wealth and its maximisation, called utilitarianism, but especially to how ones wealth compares to that of acquaintances, i.e. egalitarianism. The influence of the comparison with respect to the perceived mean has been clarified in the quantitative work [10] of the Economics Nobel laureates Kahneman e Tversky.

We thus proposed [3] to introduce a new dimension in voting theory which is precisely the standard deviation of the distances:

$$\sigma(c) = \sqrt{\frac{1}{N} \sum_{i=1}^{N} [d(v_i, c) - \mu(c)]^2}.$$

This measures the inequality in satisfaction, and allows us to have an extra criterion to select among possibilities, namely an *egalitarian criterion*. We can compute the mean distance μ and the standard deviation of the distances σ for all possible outcomes of the election (all possible rankings) and plot them in two dimensions.

For the previous example, we obtain:

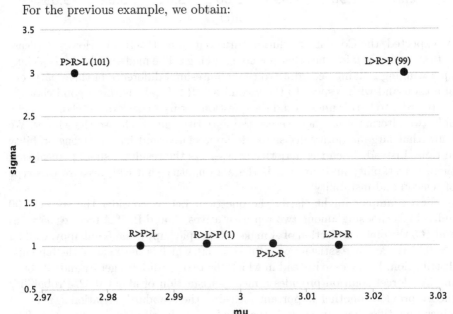

The figure clearly displays that the selection based only on the *mean* operates on infinitesimal quantities (horizontal axis) and appears to be basically arbitrary with respect to small fluctuations. The vertical axis, however, corresponding to the standard deviation, discriminates much better between possible solutions. Therefore one could consider a different choice, namely the solution $R > P > L$, which has a standard deviation three times smaller than the one emerging from the Condorcet criterion $(P > R > L)$ and that is likely going to exhibit a higher stability. We have purposely left the concept of stability as a purely intuitive one here. For details please see the original paper [3], which demonstrates through subsampling that points of low standard deviation are more stable with respect to small fluctuations in the votes cast.

3   Egalitarian Voting in Simulations

To further test the newly introduced method in more realistic settings, we generate synthetic votes from larger populations with various polarisation degrees. Our method is then applied to the resulting votes. The aim is to understand the role of the egalitarian dimension (σ), how this depends on the polarisation of the population, and how existing *heuristic voting methods* (Schulze, Tideman, Borda, Copeland [1]) compare among themselves with respect to σ.

3.1   Generating Synthetic Votes

In order to generate the ranked ballots for each voter, we first generate a set of ratings for each candidate, which we then use to rank them. We fix the number of candidates to $C = 5$ (A, B, C, D, E) and the number of voters to $N = 10000$. A recent analysis of ratings given by voters to real political candidates, in an online experiment [6], showed that, in general, voters tend to rate a few candidates very well, and many candidates very low, with an exponential distribution of ratings between the two extremes. We take this into account and try to reproduce the distribution of ratings observed in this real experiment.

Ratings are distributed in the interval $[-1, 1]$, with a positive rating corresponding to a positive opinion of the candidate. We assume that voters support two opposing parties, we call them Party 1 and Party 2. We consider the candidates A, B, C, D, E, to be ordered by the degree of popularity in the two parties. That means A is the first favoured candidate in Party 1 and E is the favoured by Party 2 voters, while B, C and D are moderate candidates in between the two parties.

Each voter gives a rating to each candidate. If a candidate is close to the voter's team, then the rating will be extracted randomly from an increasing exponential distribution that peaks at $+1$. If, on the contrary, the candidate belongs from the other side of the spectrum, the rating is extracted randomly from a decreasing exponential, peaking at -1. The steepness of the distribution is controlled by a rate parameter which is positive (in the first case) or negative (in the second), and changes from candidates A to E. This results in most ratings with values close to ± 1 and some in between.

Figure 1 shows a histogram of all ratings obtained after random sampling, for an example simulation, where 50% of voters are from Party 1 and the rest from the Party 2. We can see that the distribution obtained is similar to that of [6], in that most votes concentrate around the ± 1 values (see Fig. 2 in [6]).

The procedure outlined above also allows for simulation of populations with various levels of radicalism. That is, a moderate voter would rate their preferred candidate $+1$, their least preferred -1, and those in the middle would get intermediate votes. On the contrary, a radical voter would rate $+1$ some candidates and -1 the rest, with no intermediate ratings for the centrist candidates.

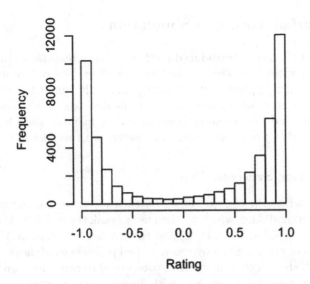

Fig. 1. Histogram of ratings for 5 candidates and 10000 voters (50000 ratings in total).

3.2 Egalitarian Voting

In the following, we generate ratings for candidates when the fraction of voters belonging to Party 1 ranges from 100% to 50% of the population, i.e., from a homogeneous to a polarised population. We consider the situation when voters from the two parties are similar in their radicalism level, i.e. the ratings they give to candidates shift from -1 to $+1$ in the same way (the rates of the exponentials are the same). From the ratings we generate the ranked ballots, that are then passed through our web application [3,4] to obtain the 2-dimensional representation of the solution space.

Figure 2 shows the solution space for the case of a completely homogeneous population, i.e. all voters come from Party 1. We can observe that the range of the utilitarian dimension (the average) is very wide, while the egalitarian dimension (the standard deviation) has a small range. Hence, in this case, it appears that the utilitarian criterion is enough to distinguish between possible solutions, i.e. to select the winner. This because, since all voters are on the same team, their satisfaction with various candidate ratings is similar. Most heuristic voting methods showed in the plot suggest $A > B > C > D > E$ as the winning ranking, which is also the winner by the Condorcet criterion.

We decrease the level of homogeneity of the population, by inserting 25% voters from Party 2, and we show the 2-dimensional space of solutions in Fig. 3. We can observe how the egalitarian dimension becomes now much wider, showing that it is most useful when the population of voters is not homogeneous in preferences. However, since a large majority of the population still comes from Party 1, the winner is again $A > B > C > D > E$, as also declared by heuristic methods.

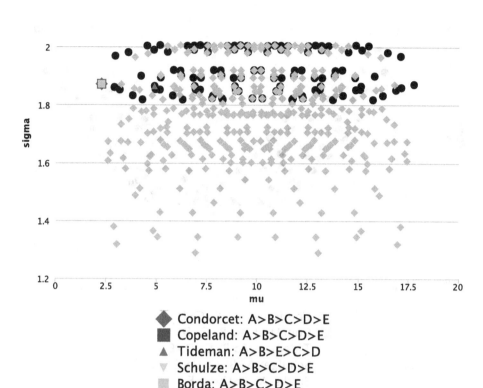

Fig. 2. Utility and egalitarianism for a homogeneous population (100% voters from Team 1). The black dots are solutions without equalities, while the grey diamonds represent the solutions with equalities among candidates.

To study the situation of maximum polarisation, we reduce further the fraction of Team 1 voters to 50%, and show the result in Fig. 4. We see that here it is the egalitarian dimension that actually dominates the plot. The range of the average distance is very small, which means this criterion has a weak discrimination power, since all possible solutions yield similar average voter satisfaction. Instead our new criterion has a very wide range, hence a very good discrimination power. We thus conclude that the egalitarian perspective is most useful when populations are heavily polarised.

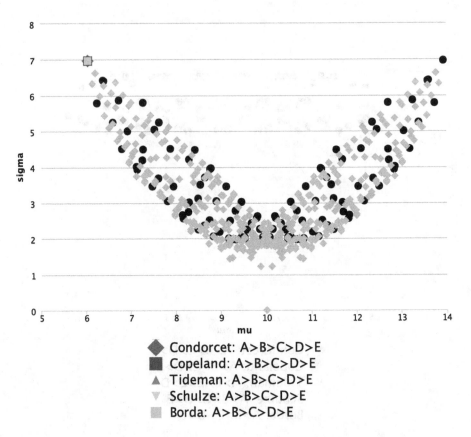

Fig. 3. Utility and egalitarianism for a population with 75% voters from Team 1.

We analyse the figure in detail and see that for all existing heuristic voting methods, the most moderate candidate (C) wins the election, which is very good given that the population is evenly divided between the two teams and voters are similarly radical. The Borda method appears to provide a better candidate ranking from the egalitarianism point of view, while preserving a high average voter satisfaction. We also observe that the point in this area of the plot with lowest σ, i.e. the most egalitarian, is the ranking with equalities $C > A = B = D = E$. This solution has $\sigma = 1.43$ and $\mu = 9.18$, compared to $\sigma = 4.45$ and $\mu = 9.12$ for the Condorcet solution. The most egalitarian solution basically summarises the result saying that, in such a balanced polarised population, candidate C is the best winning choice, while any ranking of the other candidates will decrease egalitarianism.

We now ask ourselves what happens if the population remains evenly split between teams, but one team (say Team 2) becomes more radical (which in a real setting could correspond to very extremist, outspoken opinions). Figure 5 shows the solution space, with the utilitarian and egalitarian criteria. We can observe

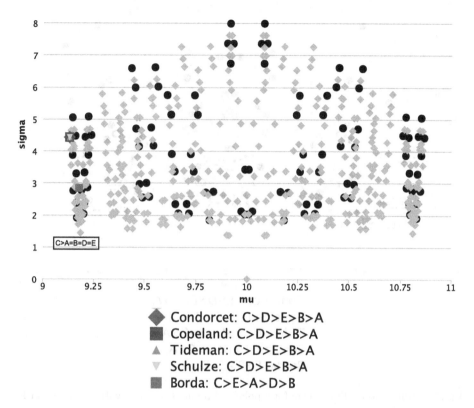

◆ Condorcet: C>D>E>B>A
■ Copeland: C>D>E>B>A
▲ Tideman: C>D>E>B>A
▽ Schulze: C>D>E>B>A
■ Borda: C>E>A>D>B

Fig. 4. Utility and egalitarianism for a polarised population (50% voters from Team 1).

that, again, the new criterion has a much higher discriminative power, since the range of values is much wider, while from the point of view of utilitarianism solutions are very close among each other. We also observe that, if we consider the existing heuristic methods, now the winning candidate is E. This means that the more radical team wins, even though the population is evenly split. The Borda solution is again more egalitarian, but the top candidate is still E.

However, if we take into account the egalitarian dimension, we observe that there are solutions with low σ and μ close to the minimum where candidate B wins instead. In fact, if we move from the Condorcet winning ranking, $E > D > B > C > A$, to the most egalitarian ranking without equalities in this area of the plot, $B > E > C > A > D$, we see that μ increases from 9.38 to 9.49 (a factor of 1.01), while σ decreases from 7.58 to 1.75 (4.33 times). We believe this is a much fairer winner, B being more moderate, since the population is evenly split between the two teams. Hence, we conclude that the introduction of this second dimension can make voting more robust to radical opinions.

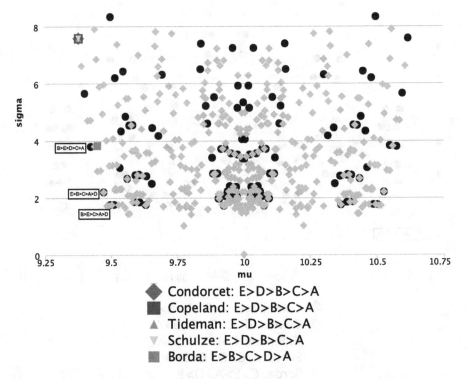

Condorcet: E>D>B>C>A
Copeland: E>D>B>C>A
Tideman: E>D>B>C>A
Schulze: E>D>B>C>A
Borda: E>B>C>D>A

Fig. 5. Utility and egalitarianism for a polarised population (50% voters from Team 1) with radical Team 2 voters.

4   Conclusion

We have reviewed how the concepts of utilitarianism and egalitarianism are both necessary to implement an aggregation criterion to select a winner in a democratic voting process. The former, introduced by Condorcet, guarantees that the total satisfaction of the voters is maximal. The latter ensures that the distribution of the satisfaction is not too uneven.

The two criteria are complementary, and we believe that both are necessary in order to select truly democratic winners. To support this claim, we analysed several scenarios where candidates come from two different parties, and the support of the voter population is distributed in various ways among the two parties. We showed that the second criterion becomes important in case of polarised populations, which is very common both in political but also in other types of social debates. Additionally, we have observed that, when using the utilitarian criterion only, radicalism in the opinions of voters can force the output of the ballots toward their positions. This effect, however, can be removed by the egalitarian criterion.

In cases of polarised populations, it may happen that by optimising utilitarianism the egalitarian dimension is not optimal, and vice versa, i.e. the two criteria are competing. This generates several optimal results, along the so-called Pareto frontier. In these situations it is the policy maker than needs to decide how to weigh the two criteria. Hence, the general landscape that emerges from this investigation is that consensus in social choice theory is not something that can be completely delegated to rules or algorithms, but the policy maker has an important role.

References

1. Börgers, C.: Mathematics of Social Choice: Voting, Compensation, and Division, Other Titles in Applied Mathematics, vol. 119. SIAM (2010). http://epubs.siam. org/doi/10.1137/1.9780898717624
2. Condorcet: Esquisse d'un tableau historique des progrès de l'esprit humain. Agasse, Paris, France (1794)
3. Contucci, P., Panizzi, E., Ricci-Tersenghi, F., Sîrbu, A.: Egalitarianism in the rank aggregation problem: a new dimension for democracy. Qual. Quantity **50**(3), 1185–1200 (2016). http://link.springer.com/10.1007/s11135-015-0197-x
4. Contucci, P., Panizzi, E., Ricci-Tersenghi, F., Sîrbu, A.: RateIt web application (2016). http://sapienzaapps.it/rateit.php
5. Gini, C.: L'uomo medio. Giornale degli economisti e rivista di statistica **48**(1), 1–24 (1914). https://www.jstor.org/stable/23223786
6. Gravino, P., Caminiti, S., Sîrbu, A., Tria, F., Servedio, V.D., Loreto, V.: Unveiling political opinion structures with a web-experiment. In: 1st International Conference on Complex Information Systems, COMPLEXIS 2016, vol. 1, pp. 39–47. SciTePress (2016). http://www.scitepress.org/DigitalLibrary/Link.aspx?doi=10. 5220/0005906300390047
7. Kemeny, J.G.: Mathematics without numbers. Daedalus **88**(4), 577–591 (1959). http://www.jstor.org/stable/20026529
8. Llull, R.: Ars notandi/Ars eleccionis/Alia ars eleccionis (1232–1315)
9. Papadimitriou, C.H.: Computational Complexity. Addison Wesley, Boston (1994). https://www.pearson.com/us/higher-education/program/Papadimitriou-Computational-Complexity/PGM94583.html
10. Tversky, A., Kahneman, D.: Judgment under uncertainty: heuristics and biases. Science **185**(4157), 1124–1131 (1974). http://science.sciencemag.org/content/185/4157/1124
11. Young, H.P.: Condorcet's theory of voting. Am. Polit. Sci. Rev. **82**(4), 1231–1244 (1988). http://www.jstor.org/stable/1961757

Knowledge Management for Democratic Governance of Socio-Technical Systems

Jeremy Pitt[1]([✉])[ID], Ada Diaconescu[2][ID], and Josiah Ober[3][ID]

[1] Department of Electrical and Electronic Engineering, Imperial College London,
London SW7 2BT, UK
j.pitt@imperial.ac.uk
[2] Departement INFRES, Télécom ParisTech, LTCI, Paris-Saclay University,
46 rue Barrault, 75013 Paris, France
ada.diaconescu@telecom-paristech.fr
[3] Department of Political Science, Stanford University, Stanford, CA 94305, USA
jober@stanford.edu

Abstract. The Digital Transformation (DX) is a broad term describing the changes and innovations brought about by the introduction of information and communication technologies into all aspects of society. One such innovation is to empower bottom-up, self-governing socio-technical systems for a range of applications. Such systems can be based on Ostrom's design principles for self-governing institutions for sustainable common-pool resource management. However, two of these principles, both focussing on self-determination, are vulnerable to distortion: either from within, as a narrow clique take control and run the system in their own, rather than the collective, interest; or from without, as an external authority constrains opportunities for self-organisation. In this chapter, we propose that one approach to maintaining 'good', 'democratic' self-governance is to appeal to the transparent and inclusive knowledge management processes that were critical to the successful and sustained period of classical Athenian democracy, and reproduce those in computational form. We review a number of emerging technologies which could provide the building blocks for democratic self-governance in socio-technical systems. However, the reproduction of analogue social processes in digital form is not seamless and not without impact on, or consequences for, society, and we also consider a number of open issues which could disrupt this proposal. We conclude with the observation that 'democracy' is not an end-state, and emphasise that self-governing socio-technical systems need responsible design and deployment of technologies that allow for continuous re-design and self-organisation.

Keywords: Socio-technical systems · Algorithmic self-governance
Knowledge management · Democracy

1 Introduction

The Digital Transformation (DX) is a broad term describing the changes and innovations brought about by the introduction of information and communica-

© Springer Nature Switzerland AG 2019
P. Contucci et al. (Eds.): *The Future of Digital Democracy*, LNCS 11300, pp. 38–61, 2019.
https://doi.org/10.1007/978-3-030-05333-8_4

tion technologies into all aspects of society, including medicine, governance, commerce, agriculture and entertainment. However, digital technologies also offer opportunities for people to form communities, and for communities to come together, to address both local and global situations – as exemplified, for example, by the transition network (http://transitionnetwork.org) or parkrun (http://www.parkrun.org.uk). Therefore one powerful innovation of DX is to empower bottom-up, self-governing socio-technical systems for a range of applications, for example in sharing economy and peer production systems [50], living and working arrangements [51], and self-supervised health management [7].

In view of the requirements for self-organisation, mutually-agreed conventional rules, and collective action underpinning all these applications, such systems can be based on Ostrom's design principles for self-governing institutions for sustainable common-pool resource management [31]. Two of these eight principles focus on aspects of self-determination: one principle (principle 3) concerns collective choice: that those who are affected by a set of rules should participate in their selection, modification and application; and another (principle 7) concerns a form of subsidiarity: the minimal recognition of the right to self-organise. However, both these principles are vulnerable to distortion, which can come from within, as a narrow clique take control and run the system in their own, rather than the collective, interest (the Iron Law of Oligarchy [26]); or from without, as an external authority constrains opportunities for self-organisation (often due to a breakdown of polycentric governance [32]).

This chapter argues that one approach to establishing and maintaining 'good', 'democratic' self-governance is, firstly, to appeal to the transparent and inclusive knowledge management processes that were critical to the successful and sustained period of classical Athenian democracy [27]; and secondly, to reproduce these processes in computational form for a self-governing socio-technical system. Accordingly, the chapter is structured as follows. We elaborate on the background and motivation in further details in Sect. 2. Concluding that there is a potential 'democracy deficit' in unrestricted self-modification, Sect. 3 reviews the knowledge management processes that underpinned classical Athenian democracy. Section 4 considers a number of emerging technologies that could provide the building blocks for democratic self-governance in socio-technical systems as the digital transformation unfolds. However, the reproduction of analogue social processes in digital form is not seamless and not without impact on, or consequences for, society, and so Sect. 5 considers a number of open issues which could disrupt this proposal. We conclude in Sect. 6 with the observation that 'democracy' is not an end-state, and emphasise that self-governing socio-technical systems need responsible design and deployment of technologies that allow for continuous re-design and self-organisation.

2 Background and Motivation

This section explores the background and motivation to this work in more detail. It starts with an overview of self-governance in socio-technical systems, suggests how self-governance might be based on the institutional design principles of Ostrom, and considers how self-governance may be disrupted or distorted by the iron law of oligarchy or a breakdown in polycentric governance.

2.1   Self-governing Socio-Technical Systems

DX is enabling a new range of socio-technical systems for the digital society and the digital economy. Examples include:

- common-pool resource management: systems which require a group of users to pool and distribute some resources, such as water or energy [31];
- peer production systems: systems in which a group of users work together without a discernible command structure, for example to produce and maintain a work of mind or provision of some service. Examples include wikipedia and open source software [50];
- sharing economy: a system for transactional arrangement in which people lease/rent assets and services to/from each other; for example cars, parking spaces, rooms, tools, and so on [24];
- workplace management: systems for managing open plan office or hot-desking arrangements with superior intervention, as a way of handling incivility in the workplace [51];
- living space management: systems for matching tenants to flatshares, and for defining and enforcing "flatmate agreements" [41];
- self-supervised health: systems picking up on recent medical practices of green prescriptions and recognition that exercise is often a more effective treatment than surgical intervention for some conditions [7].

There is, of course, some blurring of the boundaries between the classification of these systems.

However, it possible to identify (at least) three common features. Firstly, these are all *rule-based systems*: they critically depend on the existence of a set of conventional, mutually-agreed and enforceable rules. Secondly, they are all *self-organising systems*: the selection, modification and enforcement of the rules are processes that must be applied by the system participants themselves. Thirdly, these are all *value-sensitive systems*: their long-term functioning is critically dependent on the collective working for the "common good", as expressed by a set of shared, congruent values (which might not be explicitly referenced by the rules themselves).

Examples of purely social systems manifesting these features are perhaps, best epitomised by the self-governing institutions of Ostrom [31].

2.2   Self-governing Institutions

Ostrom's fieldwork identified numerous cases of successful (sustainable) common-pool resource management, across history and geography, and scales of time (i.e. several generations) and space (from local arrangements to regional agreements). This was counter to arguments based on the zero-contribution thesis [29] and the tragedy of the commons [15], which suggested that large-scale long-term collective action could not occur without coercion or the inevitable depletion of a shared resource. Ostrom attributed such 'success stories' to the 'evolution' of rulesets (or institutions) which proscribed or prescribed rights, actions, duties, roles, etc. regarding provision to and appropriation from the common-pool.

However, "evolving" a set of rules was not a sufficient condition for sustainability. Ostrom then observed that where the rules were successful, the institutions had eight common features[1], some of which were absent in situations which were unable to sustain the resource. Therefore, in one further step, Ostrom suggested that, faced with a collective action situation, if we know what features of a successful institution are, then don't rely on 'evolution' to produce the desired system, *design* an institution with those features. This was formalised in terms of eight institutional design principles (see Appendix A) and codified in the IAD methodology (Institutional Analysis and Design).

Recent work has attempted to re-express the design principles in algorithmic form using computational logic [45], giving rise to executable specifications of self-governance for electronic institutions. The intended application of electronic institutions was decentralised resource allocation in distributed systems, especially of common-pool resources (e.g. in sensor networks where nodes pool computing and communication resources, such as memory, bandwidth, cpu time, battery power, etc.). However, the same approach could apply to socio-technical systems composed of both people and software, for example community energy systems with both prosumers and "smart" meters. However, this approach exposes the system to a number of potential vulnerabilities.

2.3   Polycentrism and the Iron Law of Oligarchy

One feature of open systems ('open' in the sense that access is unconstrained) with conventional rules is the expectation of error. From one point of view, this can be an advantage, from the flexibility offered by forgiveness and the principled violation of policy [56], to the opportunities for innovation that come with unexpected variations of rule. From another point of view, openness may also admit undesirable behaviour, from wilful malpractice to sheer malice.

One type of wilful practice of particular concern is the appropriation of 'power' by a dominant clique, who then run the system in their own benefits, rather than the collective interest or the common good. In sociology, this malpractice is referred to as the iron law of oligarchy [26], which states that any self-organising system, no matter how democratically it is originally founded and constituted, inevitably ends up being run by an oligarchy (rule by a few in their own self-interest).

---

[1] Ostrom's eight common features of institutions are: lear boundaries, rule-environment congruence, participation in collective choice, monitoring and enforcement, graduated sanctions, fast and cheap dispute resolution, recognition of minimal rights to self-organise, nested enterprises—see [31] for details.

This is a distortion of a self-governing institution that comes from within. However, self-governing institutions can also be distorted by pressures form without. This can occur in large-scale systems with nested enterprises, which violate Ostrom's seventh principle (minimal recognition of the right to self-organise by external authorities). One source of failure at larger scales has been breakdown of polycentrism: i.e. the recognition that there are multiple decision-making stakeholders with possibly conflicting objectives, even if they all have a common interest in the maintenance of the ecosystem.

Therefore, the challenge is to design *self-governing socio-technical systems* which are democratically founded and constituted *ab origine*, and have a concept of *digital citizenship* that is correlated with civic participation in processes of self-determination. These systems should support appropriate error-handling as well as provide resistance to the iron law of oligarchy and respect polycentrism in nested enterprises. We propose that one source for solutions to this challenge is a study of classical Athenian democracy [27] (although see also [28] for addressing the issue of achieving cooperation at large scales without a controller).

3 Knowledge Management in Classical Athens

It has been shown that Athenian democracy, on a number of independent metrics, massively outperformed its rival city states, economically, architecturally, militarily, and diplomatically; despite a relative parity in territorial size, population density, cultural development, and availability of mineral resources [27]. The exceptional success of Athenian democracy was attributed to the greater social benefits derived from higher levels of cooperation. This in turn was based on the Athenians' superior capacity for resolving public collective action problems, which itself was a product of special features of their participatory and deliberation model of self-governance. One of the most important of these special features was the distinctive Athenian system for *organising useful knowledge*.

Suppose $\mathcal{I}$ is an institution attempting to solve some collective action problem facing the set of individuals who are members of $\mathcal{I}$. $\mathcal{I}$ itself is an abstraction, and – notwithstanding the legal notion of *corporate personhood* – does not exist as an entity capable of 'physical' action. Instead, it relies on *institutionalised power* [18] to assert institutional facts, i.e. the performance by a designated member occupying an identified role of a contextualised action with conventional significance, which *counts as* an assertion that the institutional fact is true. Then there are, essentially, three epistemic issues relating the abstract notion of $\mathcal{I}$ to the concrete set of individuals – $\mathcal{I}$ans say:

[1] Collective decision-making: how does $\mathcal{I}$ know what $\mathcal{I}$ans know?
[2] Collective coordination: how do $\mathcal{I}$ans do what $\mathcal{I}$ decides (or intends) to do?
[3] Collective 'memory': how does $\mathcal{I}$ record or remember what $\mathcal{I}$ans did (successfully)?

Ober's analysis is that the Athenians developed highly effective, transparent and interdependent epistemic processes for dealing with each of these problems, respectively, i.e. *knowledge aggregation*, by which dynamic knowledge, created by and between citizens, was used to select the 'right' course of action that 'best' represented or served their shared values; *knowledge alignment*, which used mutual knowledge to coordinate people's actions in successfully satisfying the chosen course of action; and *knowledge codification*, which standardised institutional structures and procedures, increasing openness and effectiveness and supporting inclusiveness, verification and accountability (see Fig. 1: note the arrows represent sequencing rather than dataflows. There are two sequences: in the inner sequence (solid arrows), knowledge aggregation precedes knowledge alignment and both processes are supported by codified knowledge (dotted arrows) to solve collective action problems (e.g. the distribution of common-pool resources). However, codified knowledge itself can be modified by a "knowledge aggregation—knowledge alignment" sequence, as represented by the outer sequence (dashed arrows), used for selecting and modifying the rules for the distribution of common-pool resources).

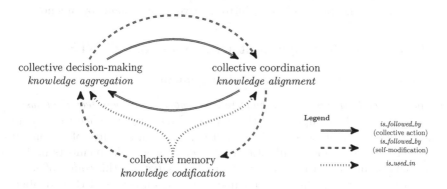

Fig. 1. Athenian knowledge management processes (adapted from [27])

Processes of knowledge aggregation proved to be highly effective in enabling a group of otherwise disparate and heterogenous individuals, when acting as (or in the context of) $\mathcal{I}$, to get the 'right' answer to a given question, in three ways: firstly, by providing incentives for knowledgeable individuals to pool their knowledge for the benefit of the group (these incentives did not have to be financial, but could be in the form of social capital (reputation) in an economy of esteem [4]); secondly, by ensuring that the cost of communication was sufficiently low to overcome the imposition of getting information from "where it was" to "where it needed to be"; and thirdly, sorting processes sifted not only false information from the true but also sifted information useful in a given context from the irrelevant.

Having reached the 'right' decision by aggregating knowledge, processes of knowledge alignment ensured that this same group of individuals with a common interest in coordinating their actions could do so effectively. Athens/Athenians then achieved high levels of coordination between individuals and institutions by intermixing four epistemic mechanisms for accurate collective coordination. These are first choice, where one agent acts and the others follow in an alignment cascade; informed leader, where one agent deemed 'more informed' is designated the leader and the others follow his/her direction; rule-following, where each agent believes there is a rule, expects others' actions to conform to that rule, and so follows the rule itself; and commitment-following, where credible pre-commitments from each are required to ensure that all will act in unison (e.g. turning up for a battle with a weapon and armour is a credible pre-commitment).

Having achieved a successful coordination by aligning common knowledge, the outcomes of both collective decision-making and collective coordination yield even greater benefit through processes of knowledge codification. This effectively creates an institutional 'memory' which can inform future behaviour of institutional members. In Athens, dynamic forms of knowledge used in the aggregation and alignment processes were codified in written laws or decrees. The Athenians also ensured that such codified knowledge was sufficiently stable to allow for confident planning, political engagement and civic education, but also sufficiently fluid to avoid ossification and allow introspective improvement by amendment.

4   Knowledge Management Processes for SG-STS

4.1   Technology for Knowledge Management

In general, a *collective action problem* in a *self-governing socio-technical system* can considered to be composed of three 'phases' (cf. Fig. 1): *collective decision-making* where the members (of the collective) agree on a course of action supposed to solve the problem; *collective coordination* where the members perform individual acts intended to satisfy or contribute to satisfying this course of action; and *collective memory* where the members use the outcomes of their deliberation and action to update the selection and coordination processes themselves, and reference them in the resolution of subsequent collective action problems. Note the cyclic nature of the inter-dependence (dual nature of knowledge as resource and instrument) means that mechanisms for inspection, introspection and intervention are also part of knowledge codification.

Our proposal is that *good* self-governance depends on the extent to which the executives of governing procedures respect the rights, interests and values of all the stakeholders: it is a question of both legitimacy [28] and correctness (deciding on the 'right' solutions to public action problems with respect to those right, interests and values, which may be in conflict between the various stakeholders). This in turn depends on how useful knowledge is organised, with a particular emphasis on knowledge management processes for aggregation, alignment and codification, and how its duality is recognised.

We also contend that delivering 'good' and 'democratic' self-governance, as well as resisting the iron law of oligarchy and supporting polycentrism, can be achieved by automating openness, transparency and inclusivity in these knowledge management processes. Furthermore, technology itself, as part of the socio-technical fabric, can be used for implementing wide-ranging strategic mechanisms underpinning these three processes, which enhance both transparency and inclusivity in several ways. This is summarised in Table 1 but these strategic mechanisms are consider in more detail in the following sub-sections.

Table 1. Knowledge management for self-governing socio-technical systems

Requirement	Process	Strategic mechanisms
Collective decision-making	*Knowledge aggregation*	Social networking, open discussion fora and computational social choice
Collective coordination	*Knowledge alignment*	Collective awareness, social capital and economy of esteem, interactive self-governance
Collective memory	*Knowledge codification*	Algorithmic self-governance, knowledge commons, institutional structuration, distributed consensus

Knowledge Aggregation

Social Networking. Social media is a catch-all term for information and communication technologies which support the dissemination of ideas and opinions and the sharing of content, often user-generated, peer-to-peer (i.e. generally eschewing and centralised production or distribution of production). The sets of dyadic relations so-formed are a computer-mediated social network, typically operating on scales far greater than pre-Internet social structures.

Online Deliberative Assemblies. An online deliberative assembly is an automated system providing advice and support for human mediators of discussion groups and decision support functions for collective decision-making applications (e.g. [12,47]). Such a system includes not only the technology for sharing resources but the algorithmic support for controlling access to those resources and running meetings according to established procedures or rules of order [49].

Computational Social Choice. It is the formal study of algorithms for mapping a set of expressed preferences onto a collective decision, for example by casting votes and applying a winner determination method (e.g. plurality, instant run-off, Borda count, etc.). Typical concerns are computational complexity, resistance to strategic behaviour, and 'legitimacy' of the result (with respect to certain abstract principles that voting procedures are expected to satisfy).

Knowledge Alignment

Collective Awareness. In any collective action situation with an agreed plan of action that is the outcome of knowledge aggregation and decision-making, people need to know what roles they occupy, what is expected of them, and how their single actions contribute to the greater whole. They must also be aware of the same data and share the same legal, social, and cultural context to interpret that data. This shared knowledge is referred to as collective awareness [37,52], and is a critical element of collaboration and coordination within communities.

Externalities. An 'externality' in economics is a benefit that is accrues, possibly to a third party, as a result of an interaction or transaction between two other actors. This is often referred to as *social capital*, and is a particular feature of organised social behaviour: that is, not content with just making up a set of rules (á l'a Ostrom) to regulate and organise behaviour, people associate a *value* with complying with those rules, which in itself triggers further pro-social behaviours, like mutual compliance, forgiveness [56], recognition of socially-beneficial contributions in consideration of distributive justice [48], and so on.

Interactive Self-governance. In the context of computer-mediated communities, this is defined as the use of visualisation, interface design and interaction affordances to ensure that the conceptual principle of self-determination – that those affected by a set of rules participate in their selection, application and modification – perceptually prominent in, and accessible through, the socio-technical interface [41].

Knowledge Codification

Algorithmic Self-governance. In contrast to algorithmic governance, which is generally conceived as the execution of rules by computer and the users accept that their actions and behaviour are constrained or enforced, algorithmic *self-governance* is based on users selecting the rules which are axiomatised executed by the computer on their behalf, for example to support fairness in the distribution of resources [39] or the compliance with mutually-agreed norms in shared working or living spaces.

Knowledge Commons. The digitalisation of information allows intellectual property to be treated as either a public good, a private good, a club good, or a common-pool resource, depending on what rules (e.g. licences, copyright laws, etc.) are use to control access and subtractability [17], where exclusion is a measure of how easy it is to allow or prevent individuals from accessing the resource, and subtractability is a measure of the extent to which one individual accessing the good subtracts from the accessibility of others. A particular form of knowledge commons is the set of rules used in algorithmic self-governance.

Institutional Structuration. The requirement here is to model, design and operate systems which conform to Ostrom's seventh and eighth institutional design principles, respectively the recognition of minimal rights to self-organise and nested enterprises. These rules concern structure and specific constraints on relationships within that structure. Therefore knowledge codification needs a representation of institutions, the resources under their jurisdiction, and the (formal, contractual) relationships between them. Understanding institutional structuration is critical to achieving polycentric self-governance [32], whereby coordinated behaviours emerge from autonomous, heterogenous and possibly competing *organisations* (i.e. not just people);

Distributed Consensus. An emerging technology for developing open systems requiring agreement (i.e. consensus on facts, events, etc.) between distributed autonomous systems is the blockchain [55]. Blockchain is essentially a protocol for building reliable, verifiable distributed ledgers. Arguably, a blockchain is simply a realisation of earlier protocols developed to solve similar problems, such as Paxos to maintain consistency in distributed databases [21], sound logical inference with inconsistent distributed knowledge bases [19], or interoperability in multi-agent systems. However, it has been critical to the development of electronic currencies, such as Bitcoin and Ripple.

The following sections consider these strategic mechanisms further, primarily in terms of offering some existing implementations or prototypes which could provide computational support for these knowledge management processes.

4.2   Knowledge Aggregation

Knowledge aggregation is concerned with open, inclusive and transparent processes for reaching the 'correct' decision; ideally always, but certainly more often than not. It is also a feature of a functional democracy that when evidence indicates that the original decision was not incorrect, it can be reviewed and rescinded, and a new course of action deliberated. This is a particular quality that distinguishes democracy as a different type of regime to majoritarian tyranny [28].

Some systems with support for strategic mechanisms for effective knowledge aggregation are the following:

Social networking. It is typical for social networking platforms to support the self-formation of (sub-)communities, such as those found in open source software development or general interest sites with domain specialisms. Similarly, video-sharing website YouTube added social networking features which enabled more tools and options for both multi-party content creation and bilateral engagement between creators and audience. This has resulted in numerous communities growing around specific channels (e.g. Bros, Nerdfighters, Sprinklerinos, etc.), some of which form online but go on to have regular meetings in the real world.

However, there are a number of pathologies associated with the ownership of social networking platforms and the means of coordination belonging to a small group of transnational organisations [11]. In contrast, one of the most promising initiatives to cede control of social networking to the users themselves was Open Mustard Seed (OMS) [16]. The foundation of OMS was a system that enabled people to share the personal data of their own choosing within a legally constituted "trust framework". All elements of the framework that accessed or aggregated that data – authentication, storage, discovery, payment, auditing, market-making and monetized "app" services – were then built according to the principles of *privacy by design* [6]. The intention was that users could establish their own social ecosystems in which shared values like mutual trust and respect for privacy were primary (supra-functional) requirements that were satisfied.

Open discussion fora. The idea of online deliberative assemblies implementing rules of order with electronic voting has been proposed and implemented in the ZENO system [47], with applications, for example, in automated decision support and computer-supported cooperative work. However, it can be argued that the proliferation of data and opinions, and its lack of structure, and the lack of filtering (enabling malpractices like trolling and spreading misinformation [30]), can actually be a hindrance to preference selection and decision-making. Therefore, some researchers have proposed that a stricter structure and a well-defined semantics be applied to 'big data' [12]. Accordingly, a number of online debating platforms and question/answer websites have emerged, based on algorithms from the theory of computational argumentation. For example, Quaestio-it (www.quaestio-it.com) is a website offering a debating infrastructure based on the modelling and analysis of social discussions and opinion exchanges.

Computational social choice. Some work developed in Social Sciences has been successfully transposed to multi-agent systems via computational social choice for distributed resource allocation and negotiation [8]. Although this research programme has largely been concerned with algorithmic complexity, and defining metrics and computational models that encourage (or compel) rational agents to determine an optimal or fair allocation of resources (i.e. mechanism design), there have also been some results in specifying and implementing robust protocols for electronic voting which ensure that the rights of the enfranchised are respected [44].

4.3   Knowledge Alignment

Having made a decision, knowledge alignment is concerned with ensuring that those people impacted by the collective situation take the necessary individual actions to resolve it. Some systems which support the strategic mechanisms for knowledge alignment are:

Collective awareness. Closely linked with knowledge aggregation, the development of collective awareness, and platforms for bringing collective awareness about, has been advocated as enhancing the enactment of sustainable strategies by the members of a community and therefore ensuring a successful resolution to a problem [52]. Collective awareness differs from mutual knowledge, and is critical to the formation of institutions, the regulation of behaviour within the context of an institution, and the direction (or selection) of actions intended to achieve a common purpose. There is also particular concern with what has been called interoceptive collective awareness [37]. By this we mean not a sense like touch or feel (i.e. a sense which induces a reactive response to an external stimulus), but rather a sense like hunger or thirst, so that it is derived from internal processes which indicate a 'physiological' condition of the collective and stimulates pro-active behaviour to promote the 'well-being' of the collective.

An initiative to promote privacy policies that correspond to user expectation is to have the users define the policies themselves through a form of collective awareness and informed consent [34]. In this approach, data collection and data protection norms are configured by the users themselves, using a collaborative participatory process of argumentation. The intention is for users to understand privacy-related documents and their implications via participatory processes, wisdom-of-the-crowds approaches and visual cues.

Externalities. Externalities in economics are consequences of commercial activities and transactions which affect third parties, without this being reflected in the price of the transaction. However, more generally, there are many externalities that are consequences of social and commercial interactions that contribute towards successful knowledge alignment (i.e. acting on the outcomes of knowledge aggregation to achieve an intended outcome). This includes norms for coordinating expectations [53], social capital [38], reputation and economies of esteem [4], and leadership (de jure or de facto) [35], all of which can contribute to successful collective action.

An algorithmic framework for representation and reasoning with electronic social capital has been developed and implemented [36]. This solution could be embedded into socio-technical systems to incentivise collective action without commodifying the qualitative pro-social properties of social capital which would reduce its effectiveness to the same level as financial leverage.

Interactive self-governance. It is a hypothesis that increasing collective awareness will increase the likelihood of successful collective action. Interactive self-governance is intended to increase collective awareness through the use of visualisation and affordances in interface design to attract and focus attention (rather than, as in some platforms, to fixate attention, e.g. though the short-term accumulation of 'likes', 'kudos', or other immediate response mechanisms ("*X is typing…*")). To test this hypothesis, a Serious Game called Social Mpower has been implemented [42], set in the context of an off-grid community energy system. The game-play effectively creates a tragedy-of-the-energy commons scenario, but it was found that increasing attention and awareness through various aspects of interface design enabled players to avoid the 'tragedy' more often. These findings were summarised as interface design principles for socio-technical systems addressing collective action situations.

Another system designed and developed to address incivility in office and residential settings is MACS [51]. MACS allowed users to specify and modify their own norms for sharing communal spaces, detecting and 'flagging' violations of those norms, and offering offenders the opportunity to apologise or make another form of reparation.

4.4 Knowledge Codification

Knowledge codification is a form of collective memory for recording what communities did and how they did it. In this way it supports both learning (of new knowledge and relationships) and re-use (efficient exploitation of existing knowledge). It partly explains Ostrom's observation that some self-governing institutions persist over several generations, when those selecting, applying and modifying the rules were not involved in the original specification and formation (education is, of course, another key factor in this process). Some systems which have used some form of knowledge codification include:

Algorithmic self-governance. Algorithmic self-governance concerns the use of computational logic to formalise self-determined governance procedures as executable protocols and programs [45]. In that work, the specification language was the event calculus [20], an action language developed to reason about the effects of actions and events. There are many 'dialects' of the event calculus, one of the most notable recent innovations is RTEC (run-time event calculus: [2]). This calculus makes is capable of processing thousands of events per second, while still being amenable to proving formal properties such as correctness and completeness, making it highly suitable for large-scale systems requiring guarantees of 'appropriate performance', at least from a procedural perspective [40].
The specification of governance procedures in executable form is an important source of knowledge codification.

Knowledge commons. It has been shown how knowledge-based systems (especially digital systems) can be treated as a provision and appropriation system, in which some users provision data or content, and some users appropriate information or knowledge [17]. It has also been shown how Ostrom's design principles and IAD (Institutional Analysis and Design) framework can be applied to designing and operating digital knowledge commons, using the same computational framework discussed above [23]. Another step is to treat rulesets for algorithmic self-governance as a knowledge commons, as a resource for learning and innovation in sustainable democratic systems [27]. An interesting example of governance procedures becoming re-usable computational resources (i.e. a convergence of algorithmic self-governance and knowledge commons) is given by the computer game Minecraft. In Minecraft, user host servers and attract other players, and although there are no specific goals to accomplish (although there is an achievement system), there is a game mode ('creative') which can be construed as a collective enterprise to construct a particular object, which can be of such a scale and complexity that it is beyond the ability of any individual player to build, but can be constructed by a community. However, the opportunity for unrestricted behaviour also enables anti-social as well as pro-social behaviour. As a consequence, bundles of governance procedures are offered as plug-ins to servers to self-organise and self-regulate players' behaviour within a server. It has been observed that there is a correspondence between the plug-in functionality and Ostrom's institutional design principles.

Institutional structuration. One of the criticisms levelled at Ostrom's research is the supposed inability to scale, and Ostrom herself was ambivalent about whether large-scale problems (i.e. at a global or planetary level) needed top-down solutions [32]. However, one possible explanation for the failure to scale is the increased likelihood that Ostrom's seventh principle – minimal recognition of the rights to self-organise – is violated as the number of organisations impacted in a collective action situation increases, and both accountability and representation decrease as the hierarchical levels in a system of nested enterprises increases.

A preliminary attempt at formalising the seventh principle can be found in [43] and a methodology for engineering complex systems is proposed in [9].

Distributed consensus. The idea of a tradeable, traceable digital token was originally intended for an electronic currency (BitCoin), the token could represent an asset of any kind, e.g. a share, an identity, a vote – or a contract, which has been referred to as a "smart" contract [14]. If the rulesets codified in, say, event calculus are construed as a 'social contract', then the convergence of RTEC and blockchain offers an interesting route to a potential 'smart social contract'.

5   Open Issues

As the implementation of Information and Communication Technology (ICT) systems for, for example, computer-supported cooperative work, access control, and electronic voting [1] have shown, the translation of social mechanisms into digital form does not necessarily follow a 'literal' process. The previous section has advocated a translation of knowledge management processes for democratic self-governance of a social system into automated support for the same processes for democratic self-governance in socio-technical systems. In this section, we consider some reservations that require deeper thought and more care, than, say, 'literal' translation, ignoring the law of unintended consequences, and relying on a naive optimism that "all will be well".

5.1   Applicability and Limitations of Self-governance

Certainly, before striving to develop viable Knowledge Management (KM) solutions for supporting self-governance systems, we should carefully establish their areas of applicability. In other words, we should differentiate problems depending on the kinds of knowledge needed to address them, and consequently identify applicable solutions for each problem type.

For instance, some problems may be 'better' addressed via the *'wisdom of the crowds'* [54] rather than by specially-assigned experts and commissions. Such cases include broad social questions requiring aggregate knowledge from a wide diversity of opinions, partial knowledge, context-dependent experiences, and experience-based perspectives. They also include cases where proposed solutions would not be validated without public consensus. Here, the ability to attract outputs from a wise crowd rather than an impulsive mob is essential.

Other types of problems may be safely assigned to automated ICT systems, relying on Big Data statistics and AI algorithms. This is the case when precision and speed are more important than customised context-aware solutions, and when loss of privacy may not be a major concern.

Another problem category requires expertise and sustained involvement from designated individuals. This concerns strategic matters where deep knowledge and experience with a particular topic is an advantage. In some cases, however, expertise may be needed but unavailable. Here, it may be difficult to establish whether assigning the task to a single individual or to everyone impacted would produce 'better' results. It may well depend on additional factors such as the necessity for absolute consensus or for quick reactions.

Indeed, agreeing on what is a 'better' approach may be an entirely relative matter, as different parties may have diverging interests.

5.2   Adapting Historic Examples to Modern Socio-Economic-Technical Contexts

To achieve increasing scalability, in terms of numbers of members and geographic distribution, societies must employ ever more sophisticated technology – i.e. to deal with ever larger-scale communication and data-processing needs. Paradoxically, replacing the traditional (non-scalable) social medium with ICT-based social interaction disrupts traditional social arrangements and requires new ones. Moreover, it raises important questions about the applicability of historic success stories, recorded from non-digital societies, to emerging socio-technical systems.

More precisely, the increasing scale enabled by ICT mediation brings several essential transformations with respect to previously analysed societies – notably in terms of numbers of members, heterogeneity of cultures and opinions, and geographic distribution. Moreover, the use of technology itself – from digital communication and knowledge management; to e-commerce and e-finance; and to the automation of essential sectors like transport, energy and manufacturing – profoundly alter the dynamics of modern societies. Continuous change at an ever-faster pace differentiates modern social environments from more stable traditional ones.

Hence, transferring KM processes that were successful in non-digital communities (such as Athens) to ICT platforms, in order to employ them to support self-governance in modern socio-technical systems, may prove a delicate process. Considering the aforementioned discrepancies between the two application domains – i.e. between traditional societies and contemporary societies relying on ICT – there is a non-negligible danger that we overlook a specific aspect that is in fact critical to the success of such (digitalised) KM processes.

Two main courses of action can help avoid such shortcomings. Firstly, we should always assume that any solution, no matter how carefully analysed and designed, will, sooner or later, reveal unanticipated shortcomings (cf. Sect. 5.3). Hence, any KM ICT platform should be designed with future adaptation in mind (e.g. "remedial democracy", or "piecemeal social engineering" [46]). This implies the provisioning of sufficient flexibility into the ICT platforms and the adaptation processes, as well as support for adaptive checks-and-balances for regulating such processes and preventing their corruption.

Secondly, when designing or adapting a KM-based solution, any examples of past successful organisations should be used as mere *inspiration* – reusing the main ideas but adapting the implementation details to the specifics of the present context; rather than replicating previously observed KM processes in different environments. Let us now look into some of the questions to be addressed for achieving such adaptation. We aim to identify the characteristics of non-digitalised societies, such as the Athenian one, that were essential (while perhaps non-obvious) to the success of their democratic systems – i.e. features that were essential to supporting their KM processes and successful self-governance; and that may be different in modern societies and hence require some adaptations.

Contrasting the social contexts of the Athenian democracy against a contemporary western democracy, some of the key questions include:

- How much time and effort, on average, did Athenian citizens (who had the right to vote) invest in knowledge acquisition, deliberation and dialectic training (underlying knowledge aggregation as discussed in Sect. 4).
  Did non-citizens living in Athens have any essential role or impact on KM?
  Comparatively, how much time and effort would career-oriented individuals afford, or be willing to invest in KM processes, within a modern highly-competitive society?
- What were the key characteristics of the Athenian social network that impacted the KM processes – in terms of network topology, communication speed, information-adjusting and filtering through direct human interaction; and how would these compare with similar aspects in modern socio-technical systems?
- How are the syntax and semantics of knowledge representations and exchanges impacted when transferred from direct human communication ('free' formats) to ICT-based media (formalised digital formats)? What is the impact on their adaptability and evolvability?
- How would the balance between transparency and privacy change when communication underlying KM processes would shift from direct human exchanges (difficult to infiltrate) within well-established community networks, to ICT-mediated exchanges (easy to intercept) within loosely-defined audiences (e.g. groups of "friends" or unverified forum members)?
- Does the speed and accuracy of communication, which differ drastically between direct human exchanges and ICT-mediated communication, have any significant impact on KM processes (e.g. knowledge aggregation and codification).

- What were the scale-related aspects that played a (perhaps non-obvious) but key role in the success Athenian KM processes?—e.g. number of citizens, geographic distribution, and consequent repeated interactions and shared experiences; hence supporting the formation of trust, leading to a relatively limited diversity of culture and enabling a common base of shared values and opinions. How would the increased dynamicity characterising modern societies, and the broad availability of extended knowledge across societies, impact the convergence of KM processes? Some relevant research directions here include proposals of subsidiarity and federal organisations (e.g. as sketched in [10]).
- How do the challenges related to keeping membership borders compare between physical environments and cyber-physical ones? – i.e. in terms of opportunity for interference with and access to the knowledge pool from illegitimate internal or external parties.

5.3   Unanticipated Consequences—"The Media Is the Message"

Since societies and their environments change over time, ICT platforms employed for mediating KM processes should be able to adapt and optimise accordingly for better congruence with shifting conditions. In such complex sociotechnical systems, evolving in complex competitive environments, the mutual effects between society and self-adaptive ICT infrastructure can never be fully predicted. Effects can range from rather obvious and short-term ones (e.g. the impact of e-communication on speed and availability), to more subtle and longer-term ones (e.g. the impacts of e-communication on inter-personal dynamics, such as the contents and expectations of exchanges, increased distraction affecting cognitive processes, and various connectivity addictions).

This was also the meaning behind Marshall McLuhan's apparent paradox – *"the media is the message"* [25] – arguing that while the content of a message may be rather obvious and immediate, the background effects of the medium via which the content is conveyed are often more subtle and longer-term, yet with significantly more dramatic *consequences* – "the personal and social consequences of any medium - that is, of any extension of ourselves - result from the new scale that is introduced into our affairs by each extension of ourselves, or by any new technology."

A society that fails to notice incipient variations (i.e. the warning signs of long-term consequences) and to pre-emptively adapt to (or avoid) predicted changes finds itself completely unprepared and forced through dramatic abrupt transformations when the actual changes do become obvious. As McLuhan points-out, "Control over change would seem to consist in moving not with it but ahead of it. Anticipation gives the power to deflect and control force". An important concern here stems from the fact that the introduction of new technologies at ever increasing paces may render anticipation of such important changes, and of their causes, impossible.

Indeed, some of the current socio-economic issues (which motivated this paper, but see also [11]) may be the early indicators of a profound change (message) ensued by the previous introduction of a new disruptive technology (medium). The technological platforms proposed in Sect. 4 may provide the necessary support for developing viable solutions for adapting to these changes. At the same time, how can we be sure that adding further new technology (i.e. for KM processes and self-governance) will provide appropriate adaptation rather than magnify disruption? Certainly, if the pace of disruption became higher than the ability of adaptation and subsequent stabilisation, there is a risk that the socio-technical-economic system subject to such disruptions would become unable to guide itself based on anticipation and pre-planning, and may be instead reduced to a mere chain of rapid post-change reactions.

While no concrete solution can fully and permanently address these significant challenges, the general direction to follow for addressing them must rely on a continuous process of observation and piece-meal transformations based on feedback; rather than on any abrupt global enforcement of unverifiable theory (e.g. [46]). Consequently, any ICT platform introduced to support KM processes for self-governance should inherently support open adaptability and evolutionary processes, enabling legitimate members to change any aspect of its processes and data formats; as well as of the changing processes themselves.

5.4   Economic Viability

The primary sources of exemplars of successful self-governance, i.e. for common-pool resource management [31] and classical *Athenian democracy* [27], come from studies of societies where KM processes mostly relied on a 'natural' social medium (i.e. with no ICT mediation). Here, KM relied on direct human communication, which required no special-purpose infrastructure or skills (even though training in dialectics helped); and hence was relatively cheap. Inherent costs came in the form of time and intellectual effort to communicate and reflect, and were shared more-or-less proportionally among participants. Feedback on the relevance of a contribution was provided immediately (e.g. by being granted attention or ignored) and outstanding involvement was rewarded by social capital (e.g. prestige).

In contrast, in digitalised societies where KM (and self-governance) processes are mediated via ICT, special-purpose ICT infrastructure must be developed and maintained, requiring significantly higher skills and costs. Any society willing to employ such techniques should be willing to pay these costs (e.g. public funds) and regulate the development processes. Alternatively, such key ICT mediation platforms would be developed exclusively by an unregulated skilled minority and/or financed by special interests, with all the risks involved (also see Sect. 5.5).

Similarly, as previously argued, continuous and open-ended adaptability is an essential feature of KM processes for successful self-governance. In "purely social" systems, all members could participate in, and implement, KM process adaptation by merely discussing and agreeing upon it. Hence, the adaptation meta-process that changed the core KM processes was inherently inclusive, relatively cheap and immediate. In socio-technical systems, this would again come at an extra financial and regulatory cost; since adapting ICT platforms requires expertise and financial resources. Moreover, unlike commonly-agreed social rules, formalised algorithmic rules are often hard-coded into ICT platforms, which, once broadly adopted and owned, become difficult and costly to replace.

To be successful over the long term, in addition to the additional costs for the actual self-governance ICT platforms, such platforms will have to be compatible with the existing socio-economic framework; and hence, at a minimum, be economically viable. Ideally, however, they would go beyond mere viability, and provide valid answers to some of today's major socio-economic questions – notably, the disruptive effects of AI and automatic control technology on the job market. For instance, ICT platforms for self-governance may be embedded into emerging socio-cyber-physical systems, such as smart grids, smart cities and the IoT, in order to ensure that those contributing to the success of these new systems (e.g. data providers and edge workers) also receive some of the benefits (e.g. share the revenues). Beyond questions of fairness, this may be essential to the long-term viability of market economies combined with democratic systems (e.g. [3, 22]). While one cannot stop the train of technological advancement by standing in its way, one can hope to catch a seat on the train, ideally in the control room, and contribute to steering its way through paths that are both sustainable and respectful of societal values.

5.5   Power Plays

As previously discussed, in digital societies, ICT platforms for KM and self-governance have to be developed and maintained by a skilled minority (rather than being accessible to all citizens). To prevent corruption – i.e. the expert minority misusing their key role – a certain level of trust, reinforced by appropriate checks-and-balances, must be set in place. The situation becomes still more difficult if critical KM platforms were financed and owned by an unregulated minority [22, 33, 57].

Generally, any sustainable democracy must permanently invest into identifying its weak-spots, which are vulnerable to corruption (i.e. Michel's iron law [26]) – whereas a minority may abuse their positions or play the system in order to acquire illegitimate power); and introducing appropriate checks-and-balances to prevent such developments. This continual vigilance becomes paramount when (frequently) introducing disruptive ICT into society, opening ever more opportunities for illegitimate power accumulation. KM and self-governance ICT platforms are no exception. Their long-term success will critically depend on the introduction of appropriate checks-and-balances that prevent them from becoming yet another illegitimate and more powerful control tool; while also keeping sufficient checks-and-balances on external interference that may neutralise it.

A more futuristic, yet not inconceivable challenge may consist in corruption that does not target the self-governing apparatus directly, but instead gains control of the very goals and values of the self-governing members. Indeed, for instance, if most members of a society were to desire profound inequality and continuous struggle for survival, then the systems that reinforced such desires would be difficult to change by direct democratic means.

Such an approach may neutralise self-governance by either corrupting available knowledge directly (e.g. by controlling the way it is produced and disseminated via ICT platforms), or, more subtly, by capitalising on the long-term side-effects of the prolonged use of pervasive ICT platforms on the individual's KM capabilities (e.g. diverse ICT causing continuous distraction and preventing the development of reflective abilities [5, 13, 25]).

6 Summary and Conclusions

To summarise, a fundamental challenge of the digital transformation is to design, develop and deploy socio-technical systems which empower 'digital citizens' to generate local solutions to collective action problems. It is our contention that this process can be suitably informed by appealing to well-documented instances of successful collective action studied in political science, notably in sustainable common-pool resource management [31] and classical Athenian democracy [27].

Therefore we try to build computational equivalents of these primary features of these systems in socio-technical systems. In previous work, we focused on the formalisation of Ostrom's institutional design principles in computational logic [45]; in this work, we have concentrated on formalising the knowledge management processes that underpinned public action in classical Athens. We have surveyed both technologies and strategic mechanisms for developing computational equivalents of these processes, but noting that the transformation of social systems into socio-technical systems is not a linear or straightforward process, nor immune to the law of unintended consequences.

In conclusion, then, if we want democratic socio-technical systems supporting models of good governance, then observing best practice in social systems is a reasonable place to start. All the same, we need to tread carefully: democracy is not an end state in itself, and so the socio-technical systems underlying the digital transformation require significantly more complex types of design (in particular design that is sensitive to 'supra-functional requirements' like (human) values), and require the capacity for *continuous* re-design and re-invention.

Moreover, the model of knowledge management for democratic self-governance, proposed here, must comprehend issues of knowledge usage and ICT application. Since neither science nor basic technologies have any inherent values ('goodness' or 'badness') – but design and generativity inherently *do* – the impacts of their particular applications onto societal values should be carefully monitored; and when necessary appropriate adaptive actions undertaken. Surely, community values might eventually come into conflict with orthodox economic ideology, or might be subverted by powerful minority interests. Considering the decisive socio-economic impacts that such ICT applications may have, one would hope that seriously considering such issues would not be too much to ask from societies whose core values and governance may be at stake.

Acknowledgements. The first author has been partially supported by the Leverhulme Trust, Research Fellowship RF-2016-451.

Appendix A: Ostrom's Institutional Design Principles

Ostrom's eight institutional design principles are [31, pp. 91–101]:

1. *Clearly defined boundaries*—"Individuals or households who have rights to withdraw resource units from the CPR must be clearly defined, as must the boundaries of the CPR itself."
2. *Congruence between appropriation and provision rules and local conditions*— "Appropriation rules restricting time, place, technology, and/or quantity of resource units are related to local conditions and to provision rules requiring labor, materials, and/or money."
3. *Collective-choice arrangements*—"Most individuals affected by the operational rules can participate in modifying the operational rules."
4. *Monitoring*—"Monitors, who actively audit CPR conditions and appropriator behaviour, are accountable to the appropriators or are the appropriators."
5. *Graduated sanctions*—"Appropriators who violate operational rules are likely to be assessed [sic] graduated sanctions (depending on the seriousness and context of the offence) by other appropriators, by officials accountable to these appropriators, or by both."
6. *Conflict-resolution mechanisms*—"Appropriators and their officials have rapid access to low-cost local arenas to resolve conflicts among appropriators or between appropriators and officials."
7. *Minimal recognition of rights to organise*—"The rights of appropriators to devise their own institutions are not challenged by external governmental authorities."
8. *Nested enterprises*—"Appropriation, provision, monitoring, enforcement, conflict resolution, and governance activities are organised in multiple layers of nested enterprises."

References

1. Appel, A.: Ceci n'est pas une urne: on the internet vote for the assemblée des français de l'etranger. Princeton University and INRIA, June 2006. http://www.cs.princeton.edu/~appel/papers/urne-fr.pdf
2. Artikis, A., Sergot, M.J., Paliouras, G.: An event calculus for event recognition. IEEE Trans. Knowl. Data Eng. **27**(4), 895–908 (2015). http://ieeexplore.ieee.org/document/6895142/
3. Bookstaber, R.: The End of Theory: Financial Crises, the Failure of Economics, and the Sweep of Human Interaction. Princeton University Press, Princeton (2017). http://press.princeton.edu/titles/10972.html
4. Brennan, G., Pettit, P.: The Economy of Esteem. An Essay on Civil and Political Society. Oxford University Press, Oxford (2005). http://global.oup.com/academic/product/the-economy-of-esteem-9780199289813
5. Carr, N.: The Shallows: What the Internet is Doing to Our Brains. W. W. Norton & Company, New York (2010). http://books.wwnorton.com/books/The-Shallows/
6. Cavoukian, A.: Privacy by design [leading edge]. IEEE Technol. Soc. Mag. **31**(4), 18–19 (2012). https://ieeexplore.ieee.org/document/6387956/

7. Cheetham, D.R., Burgess, L., Ellis, M., Williams, A., Greenhalgh, R., Davies, A.: Does supervised exercise offer adjuvant benefit over exercise advice alone for the treatment of intermittent claudication? A randomised trial. Eur. J. Vasc. Endovasc. Surg. **27**(1), 17–23 (2004). http://www.sciencedirect.com/science/article/pii/S1078588403004702
8. Chevaleyre, Y., Endriss, U., Lang, J., Maudet, N.: A short introduction to computational social choice. In: van Leeuwen, J., Italiano, G.F., van der Hoek, W., Meinel, C., Sack, H., Plášil, F. (eds.) SOFSEM 2007. LNCS, vol. 4362, pp. 51–69. Springer, Heidelberg (2007). https://doi.org/10.1007/978-3-540-69507-3_4
9. Diaconescu, A., Frey, S., Müller-Schloer, C., Pitt, J., Tomforde, S.: Goal-oriented holonics for complex system (self-)integration: concepts and case studies. In: 10th IEEE International Conference on Self-adaptive and Self-organizing Systems SASO, pp. 100–109 (2016). http://ieeexplore.ieee.org/document/7774391/
10. Diaconescu, A., Pitt, J.: Holonic institutions for multi-scale polycentric self-governance. In: Ghose, A., Oren, N., Telang, P., Thangarajah, J. (eds.) COIN 2014. LNCS (LNAI), vol. 9372, pp. 19–35. Springer, Cham (2015). https://doi.org/10.1007/978-3-319-25420-3_2
11. Diaconescu, A., Pitt, J.: Technological impacts in socio-technical communities: values and pathologies. IEEE Technol. Soc. Mag. **36**(3), 63–71 (2017). http://ieeexplore.ieee.org/document/8038129/
12. Evripidou, A., Toni, F.: Quaestio-it.com: a social intelligent debating platform. J. Dec. Syst. **23**(3), 333–349 (2014). http://www.tandfonline.com/doi/10.1080/12460125.2014.886496
13. Franklin, U.: The Real World of Technology. CBC Massey Lectures Series. Anansi Press, Toronto (1992)
14. Frantz, C., Nowostawski, M.: From institutions to code: towards automated generation of smart contracts. In: 2016 IEEE 1st International Workshops on Foundations and Applications of Self* Systems (FAS*W), Augsburg, Germany, 12–16 September 2016, pp. 210–215 (2016). http://ieeexplore.ieee.org/document/7789470/
15. Hardin, G.: The tragedy of the commons. Science **162**(3859), 1243–1248 (1968). http://science.sciencemag.org/content/162/3859/1243
16. Hardjono, T., Deegan, P., Clippinger, J.H.: Social use cases for the ID3 open mustard seed platform. IEEE Technol. Soc. Mag. **33**(3), 48–54 (2014). http://ieeexplore.ieee.org/document/6901333/
17. Hess, C., Ostrom, E.: Understanding Knowledge as a Commons. MIT Press, Cambridge (2006). http://mitpress.mit.edu/books/understanding-knowledge-commons
18. Jones, A.J., Sergot, M.: A formal characterisation of institutionalised power. Logic J. IGPL **4**(3), 427–443 (1996). http://academic.oup.com/jigpal/article-abstract/4/3/427/708084
19. Kowalski, R.: Logic-based open systems. In: Representation and Reasoning, pp. 125–134 (1988)
20. Kowalski, R., Sergot, M.: A logic-based calculus of events. New Gener. Comput. **4**(1), 67–95 (1986). http://link.springer.com/10.1007/BF03037383
21. Lamport, L.: The part-time parliament. ACM Trans. Comput. Syst. **16**(2), 133–169 (1998). http://dl.acm.org/citation.cfm?id=279229
22. Lanier, J.: Who Owns the Future?. Simon & Schuster, New York (2013). http://www.simonandschuster.com/books/Who-Owns-the-Future/Jaron-Lanier/9781451654974
23. Macbeth, S., Pitt, J.: Self-organising management of user-generated data and knowledge. Knowl. Eng. Rev. **30**(3), 237–264 (2015). http://doi.org/10.1017/S026988891400023X

24. Malhotra, A., Van Alstyne, M.: The dark side of the sharing economy... and how to lighten it. Commun. ACM **57**(11), 24–27 (2014). http://dl.acm.org/citation.cfm?doid=2668893

25. McLuhan, M.: Understanding Media: The Extensions of Man. McGraw Hill, New York (1964)

26. Michels, R.: Political Parties: A Sociological Study of the Oligarchical Tendencies of Modern Democracy. Hearst's International Library Co., New York (1915)

27. Ober, J.: Democracy and Knowledge. Innovation and Learning in Classical Athens. Princeton University Press, Princeton (2008). http://press.princeton.edu/titles/8742.html

28. Ober, J.: Demopolis: Democracy Before Liberalism in Theory and Practice. Cambridge University Press, Cambridge (2017). http://doi.org/10.1017/9781108226790

29. Olson, M.: The Logic of Collective Action. Harvard University Press, Cambridge (1965). http://www.hup.harvard.edu/catalog.php?isbn=9780674537514

30. Oreskes, N., Conway, E.M.: Merchants of Doubt: How a Handful of Scientists Obscured the Truth on Issues from Tobacco Smoke to Global Warming. Bloomsbury Press, London (2010). http://www.bloomsbury.com/uk/merchants-of-doubt-9781596916104/

31. Ostrom, E.: Governing the Commons. Cambridge University Press, Cambridge (1990). http://www.cambridge.org/core_title/gb/478715

32. Ostrom, E.: Beyond markets and states: polycentric governance of complex economic systems. Am. Econ. Rev. **100**(3), 641–672 (2010). http://www.jstor.org/stable/27871226

33. Pasquale, F.: Black Box Society. The Secret Algorithms that Control Money and Information. Harvard University Press, Cambridge (2015). http://www.hup.harvard.edu/catalog.php?isbn=9780674368279

34. Patkos, T., et al.: Privacy-by-norms privacy expectations in online interactions. In: IEEE International Conference on Self-adaptive and Self-organizing Systems SASO Workshops, pp. 1–6 (2015). http://ieeexplore.ieee.org/document/7306528/

35. Perret, C., Powers, S., Hart, E.: Emergence of hierarchy from the evolution of individual influence in an agent-based model. In: ECAL 2017: The Fourteenth European Conference on Artificial Life (2017). http://www.mitpressjournals.org/doi/abs/10.1162/isal_a_058

36. Petruzzi, P.E., Pitt, J., Busquets, D.: Electronic social capital for self-organising multi-agent systems. ACM Trans. Auton. Adapt. Syst. **12**(3), 13:1–13:25 (2017). http://dl.acm.org/citation.cfm?id=3124642

37. Pitt, J., et al.: Transforming big data into collective awareness. IEEE Comput. **46**(6), 40–45 (2013)

38. Pitt, J., Nowak, A.: The reinvention of social capital for socio-technical systems. IEEE Technol. Soc. Mag. **33**(1), 27–33 (2014)

39. Pitt, J., Busquets, D., Macbeth, S.: Distributive justice for self-organised common-pool resource management. ACM Trans. Auton. Adapt. Syst. **9**(3), 14:1–14:39 (2014). http://dl.acm.org/citation.cfm?id=2629567

40. Pitt, J., Busquets, D., Riveret, R.: Procedural justice and 'fitness for purpose' of self-organising electronic institutions. In: Boella, G., Elkind, E., Savarimuthu, B.T.R., Dignum, F., Purvis, M.K. (eds.) PRIMA 2013. LNCS (LNAI), vol. 8291, pp. 260–275. Springer, Heidelberg (2013). https://doi.org/10.1007/978-3-642-44927-7_18

41. Pitt, J., Diaconescu, A.: Interactive self-governance and value-sensitive design for self-organising socio-technical systems. In: FAS* Workshop Proceedings: SASOST (2016). http://ieeexplore.ieee.org/document/7789436/

42. Pitt, J., Diaconescu, A., Bourazeri, A.: Democratisation of the SmartGrid and the active participation of prosumers. In: IEEE 26th International Symposium on Industrial Electronics (ISIE) (2017). http://ieeexplore.ieee.org/document/8001505/

43. Pitt, J., Jiang, J., Diaconescu, A.: On the minimal recognition of rights in holonic institutions. In: Cranefield, S., Mahmoud, S., Padget, J., Rocha, A.P. (eds.) COIN -2016. LNCS (LNAI), vol. 10315, pp. 149–169. Springer, Cham (2017). https://doi.org/10.1007/978-3-319-66595-5_9

44. Pitt, J., Kamara, L., Sergot, M., Artikis, A.: Voting in multi-agent systems. Comput. J. **49**(2), 156–170 (2006). https://ieeexplore.ieee.org/document/8139364/

45. Pitt, J., Schaumeier, J., Artikis, A.: Axiomatisation of socio-economic principles for self-organising institutions: concepts, experiments and challenges. ACM Trans. Auton. Adapt. Syst. **7**(4), 39:1–39:39 (2012). http://dl.acm.org/citation.cfm?id=2382575

46. Popper, K.: The Open Society and Its Enemies (Merged Edition). Princeton University Press, Princeton (2013 [1945])

47. Prakken, H., Gordon, T.F.: Rules of order for electronic group decision making – a formalization methodology. In: Padget, J.A. (ed.) Collaboration between Human and Artificial Societies 1997. LNCS (LNAI), vol. 1624, pp. 246–263. Springer, Heidelberg (1999). https://doi.org/10.1007/10703260_15

48. Rescher, N.: Distributive Justice. Bobbs-Merrill, Indianapolis (1966)

49. Robert, S.C., Robert, H., Evans, W.J., Honemann, D.H., J., B.T.: Robert's Rules of Order, Newly Revised, 10th edn. Perseus Publishing, Cambridge, MA (2000)

50. Rychwalska, A., Roszczyńska-Kurasińska, M.: Value sensitive design for peer production systems: mediating social interactions. IEEE Technol. Soc. Mag. **36**(3), 48–55 (2017). http://ieeexplore.ieee.org/document/8038116/

51. Santos, M.S., Pitt, J.: Emotions and norms in shared spaces. In: Balke, T., Dignum, F., van Riemsdijk, M.B., Chopra, A.K. (eds.) COIN 2013. LNCS (LNAI), vol. 8386, pp. 157–176. Springer, Cham (2014). https://doi.org/10.1007/978-3-319-07314-9_9

52. Sestini, F.: Collective awareness platforms: engines for sustainability and ethics. IEEE Technol. Soc. Mag. **31**(4), 54–62 (2012). http://ieeexplore.ieee.org/document/6387972/

53. Southwood, N., Eriksson, L.: Norms and conventions. Philos. Explor. **14**(2), 195–217 (2011). http://www.tandfonline.com/doi/abs/10.1080/13869795.2011.569748

54. Surowiecki, J.: The Wisdom of Crowds. Little, Brown, Boston (2004)

55. Ulieru, M.: Blockchain and the real sharing economy: 'uberisation' demystified. LinkedIn, September 2016. http://www.linkedin.com/pulse/blockchain-real-sharing-economy-uberisation-dr-mihaela-ulieru/

56. Vasalou, A., Hopfensitz, A., Pitt, J.: In praise of forgiveness: ways for repairing trust breakdowns in one-off online interactions. Int. J. Hum.-Comput. Stud. **66**(6), 466–480 (2008). http://www.sciencedirect.com/science/article/pii/S1071581908000232

57. Zuboff, S.: Big other: surveillance capitalism and the prospects of an information civilization. J. Inf. Technol. **30**(1), 75–89 (2015). http://link.springer.com/article/10.1057/jit.2015.5

The Problematic Relationship Between Trust and Democracy; Its Crisis and Web Dangers and Promises

Cristiano Castelfranchi and Rino Falcone[✉]

Istituto di Scienze e Tecnologie della Cognizione (ISTC), CNR, Rome, Italy
{cristiano.castelfranchi,rino.falcone}@istc.cnr.it

Abstract. In this chapter we discuss the revolution of digital democracy (a.k.a. on-line democracy), by arguing that it should integrate (rather than replace) representative democracy based on computational tools and platforms, and that the relationship between people and their representatives and institutions remains absolutely crucial to democracy as a *bilateral trust relation*.

Keywords: On-line democracy · Delegation · Trust

1 Premise

Our thesis is that:

(i) On-line Democracy can be a great and positive revolution, however it cannot replace at all levels "representative" democracy (by becoming "direct" or "deliberative" democracy) and thus the need for "intermediation", but should integrate it. Of course, also this *intermediation has to be rethought and redefined* on the basis of these *new electronic instruments and communities*, but its function and role remain, in our view, essential.

(ii) This maintains as absolutely crucial in democracy the *bilateral trust relation* between people and their representatives and institutions; thus, it makes crucial how new web-infrastructure is contributing to the (not accidental) discredit of democracy and collapse of trust, and, on the contrary, could contribute to a new trust building and support.

The increasing and, in a sense, structural crisis of representative democracies is due to an historically-new conflict between such political regime and economic powers and strategies, and on a serious disempowerment of political national institutions. However, for such reason – together with other social and cultural dynamics – it also is a dramatic crisis of the *people trust in their representatives, parties, and political government. Representation* implies *delegation* and *reliance*: "they" are in charge of taking care of "our" interests; even beyond what we can understand, expect, or require (necessary "tutelary" role with its paternalistic risks).

© Springer Nature Switzerland AG 2019
P. Contucci et al. (Eds.): *The Future of Digital Democracy*, LNCS 11300, pp. 62–82, 2019.
https://doi.org/10.1007/978-3-030-05333-8_5

On the basis of our model of *trust* [4] we explain why people feels "betrayed". They are doubly disappointed: *(a)* by the non-solution of such a long economic and social crisis and the worsening of their life conditions (where politicians seem either unable or insensible about); *(b)* by the feeling that the locus of decisions is much farther than before (like in Nation vs. Europe, etc.), and that real decision powers are out of democratic control (banks, multinational private organisations, etc.). Yet, without trust and felt trustworthiness and counting-on the delegated other, democracy is no longer really "representative"; it is some sort of expropriation of "demos"' power and will; some distancing of political class (intended as the decision-makers) from problems and interests of people.

Is the Web (support for establishing communities, for information apparently without limits, for discussion, for voting, for proposal and petitions, etc.) a possible revitalisation of democracy and of the voice and role of citizens? Without any "organisation" of them? Without any "intermediation"? Or, instead, it is mainly a font of a political drift: fake news, illusion to know and understand, non-real "discussions" and "decisions", mainly protests, demagogy, mass psychology; mainly expression of fomented rage. Is "direct/deliberative" democracy possible, and at which layer? Does a social net work as an "assembly"?

Moreover, should "representatives" just be obeying executors of specific bottom up "orders"? Or, should they have some autonomy and consequent "responsibility"?[1] Is the Web (at least in its current state and its working) encouraging the biased view of political fight as "we" (undifferentiated people) against "them" (the "caste", the power representatives); with no distinction between conflicts of interests of classes, categories, genders, sub-communities? Which is the difference between *direct vs. participatory democracy*? Could a good use of the Web ground a much more "participatory" democracy? Is full transparency really possible and useful in political government, or, do they need some "secret"? We will stress the limit of *transparency* (a misleading current ideology) and what should really be made visible in politics thanks to digital technology.

1.1 Participatory vs. Deliberative

For a thorough review and discussion of the literature on *participatory* and *deliberative democracy*, see [13]. Since we cannot discuss all the related philosophical and political tradition here[2], we just remark two issues.

- On the one side, the use of the term "deliberative" is not exactly the same of our own – more common sense – use, where people directly decide (by

---

[1] On *representative democracy* theory and nature, see [23].

[2] Of course, references on the very rich and important political and philosophical literature on the theory of democracy and its problems should be extended considerably; but this is not the right place—and not our competence, indeed. We just pay homage to a very remarkable thinker, Norberto Bobbio, as well as to his defence and criticism to democracy [2]. Moreover, on the specific issue of deliberative democracy – as a critical view of other conceptions of democracy – we would like to mention (apart from that review) Jurgen Habermas' famous work [15].

voting) on political issues. We agree that a good "participatory" democracy necessarily implies some direct decision on relevant issues, at some level (for example, local level, specific competence or work domain, etc.), and we also agree that "deliberative" democracy is not just voting: the most relevant aspect is a true discussion, argumentation, re-orientation etc. However, we claim that a *clear distinction* should be maintained, since "deliberative" or "direct" democracy is not the good solution (even with good discussion levels) to be applied at any level of social order and of political decision; while some form of "participation" is good. Some level and domain of "representative" and non-directed democracy is crucial for common interests, for rights and minorities protection, for good compromises.

– On the other side, let us say that the spirit of this work (and literature) seems rather influenced by a (either naïve or hypocritical) ideology: the idea that the role of the State, the reason for and the mission of political government (and even the reason for "societies") is *common good*; with some denial of material *conflict of interests* of different classes or social groups, and that there is a "war" (in Keynes's rather than in Lenin's terms) [20] to be managed, not only for avoiding violence or rules and rights violations but for avoiding increasing unbalanced results: exploitation, domination, oppression, and misery. It is a matter of substance, not just of manners; it is matter of *who and why and how is prevailing*, not of the fact that they (for irrational reasons!) do not realise that they have a common interest, that they should agree instead of fighting. Prevention of strong social fights is the presupposition of a working democracy: it has to be able to transform in regulated political struggle those profound conflicts that live within society; but also to be the way for social progress, equality and equity, expansions of "capabilities" (in Sen's sense), instruction, health, not-exploitation, and so on.

Our claims are in favour of strongly "participatory" democracy (improved by the net) in which is relevant, clear, well-defined, and bounded the role of the intermediation (intermediate bodies), with some room also for decentralised and direct decisions, but against the so called "direct" democracy replacing representative and mediating institutions.

In their interesting work, Helbing and Klauser [16] suggest a specific platform-based approach to engage people in the deliberation process. We converge enough with their analysis and recommendations, but not with their strong optimism and technologically-oriented perspective. First, one should seriously consider the risks and dangers of current trends in Digital Democracy. They cite the view of Dhruva Jaishankar [17] (... *digital democracy in the evil that makes our world ungovernable*), yet they claim that such an alert is "misleading", since *digital democracy – if properly understood – is the most promising way to build prosperous societies*. One might agree, yet:

(i) "if properly understood" while there is not very much evidence that it is properly understood and used;

(ii) moreover: is it just a matter of understanding? Or, are there specific interests for a distorted and demagogic use of digital democracy and of their inflated majorities?

The authors, in fact, later point out one serious danger of digitalisation:

> Some commenters suggest that voters cannot handle this complexity – they would be easily manipulable and lean towards populist and inadequate solutions.

This in favour of a hidden, centralised, top-down, and Big Data/AI-based control.

> The long-term consequences of centralized top-down control could be devastating due to a loss of socio-economic diversity and resilience... Centralized top-down optimization may be a proper paradigm for companies or supply chains, but complex societies need pluralism and combinatorial innovation to thrive.

And they conclude (and we agree on that) that:

> Overall, to achieve culturally fitting, sustainable and legitimate results that leverage the benefits of complexity and diversity, it is crucial to *move from a government paradigm based on power* [and reinforcing current powers] *to a paradigm based on empowerment.* Combining smart technologies with smart citizens is the recipe to create smarter societies.

However, their "solution" is quite optimistic and reductive:

> This can be reached by creating Massive Open Online Deliberation Platforms (MOODs), which allow *all interest groups* to put their *arguments* on a particular subject *on a virtual table, where they can be structured into different points of view.*

Or, in the words of Landa and Meirowitz [19]:

> In revealing correct, fuller, or simply better organized information, deliberation provides an opportunity for participants to arrive at more considered judgments themselves and to affect collective decision making by influencing the judgments of others.

As we said above, we do agree with that kind of "framing" of participatory platforms, however it is not primarily a technological problem; instead, it is a *strictly-political problem*: who will like such a kind of digital democratic and more inclusive support aimed at real discussion, understanding, critical thinking, compromises, complexity and diversity and pluralism, different respected views and solutions, minorities, etc.? Why do not use other theatrical forms of digital consultation, multitude activation, opinion aggregation, emotional reactions and hates..., precisely in order to support dominant interests and powers? This probably is the more "natural" (both spontaneous and manipulated) trend. The problem is how to politically fight against such a degeneration of a simulated democracy.

1.2   Trust Not Just Useful but Intrinsic in Democracy

Obviously, some form of trust is very relevant in *any kind of political regime*. In fact, any form of domination – even dictatorship – prefers not to count just on submission based on surrender and resignation, or just on spontaneous subjection, but rather on some positive and supporting attitude, like faith in the leader (Mussolini, Mao, Castro, etc.) or in the "ideals" of the regime (like fascism ideology, etc.). This obviously makes the domination much more stable, less hard and costly, more participated and controlled from the bottom, and so on. However, this is just the best possible condition (people support and fanaticism) but it is not *intrinsic* in the idea of domination or dictatorship. On the other hand, our claim is that "representative" democracy intrinsically, *structurally* requires a trust relation from the governed towards the governors (and possibly vice versa); otherwise, it cannot work—it is in a structural crisis.

(a) We want to clarify here how trust applied to political field is better represented if articulated, on the one side, towards the institutions and decision-making and government systems and on the other side, towards direct and indirect representatives. Not always this distinction is clear, perceivable and aware. But we are interested in analysing when the attitude of trust undergoes a differentiation on this basis. Perceived trustworthiness of a given political subject is its main "capital" to be acquired and preserved; and it is not a generic community "trust capital", it is a competitive resource and object of conflict [5]. "Trust capital" as a supporting and solidarity network is not at all a requirement of democracy within the undifferentiated "people", but it just is a requirement within a given organisation, party, movement.

(b) Another relevant concept that has to be analysed is the real sense of the political representation. In the classical vision, a "representative" does not mean "spokesperson", a monitored "executor" of specific advices, but people's *delegate* to take care of some complex and long-term objectives, of some values; with some degree of autonomy (and thus of responsibility and accountability) for studying and understanding, for finding possible solutions, etc. Of course, it is expected that these solutions and hypothesis are coherent with (and internal to) the set of values and principles declared and shared with the political and social community expressing those representative. The "represented" people in order to "delegate" have to consider they trustworthy both for their competence and capabilities, and for their honest willingness, determination, values, sincere care of group/class interests. This is not optional and better; it is substantial for that kind of relation.[3] It is what we call "open delegation": assigning a mission not a specified task to be executed (Sect. 2). Obviously, in some more "direct" interpretations of the political relationship between representative and represented, or in some circumstances the delegation is considered more constraining and in some cases even strictly "executive", especially after a vote or consultation.

---

[3] Some specific form of trust is structurally necessary, *intrinsic* also for a working cooperation/organisation or in market.

(c) Moreover, in our trust theory a crucial assumption is that trust in somebody has an "object" (O), it is "about" and "for" something (what I intend to obtain, achieve; what I delegate to the other); it is due to the evaluation of specific "qualities" of the trustee useful for O; and it is context dependent, not always "general". One should not say "X trusts Y", but "X trusts Y as for O" (but not for O') and "as for Y being...", and in those conditions, context. In political trust it is relevant to reflect on that: which are the needed qualities, the "virtues" we search in our representatives or we are disappointed about? For example, now – due to the scandalmongering distortion of media and of political debate – for people the (more and more) unique criteria for trust is "honesty", "non-corruption" (not belonging to the "caste" which is entirely corrupted!), and aggressiveness and visibility; not at all "competence" or "political experience" or "strong ideality" or "good arguing". Yet honesty can only be a prerequisite for other relevant and essential attributions: those necessary to realise the common and shared goals. And in several democratic countries it holds that "non-corruption" is a good but an additional (not prior) factor, while the primary requirement is that s/he will be loyal in her/his commitment with us and able to realise our interests.

2   "Delegation", "Reliance", Trust, and Commitment

"Delegation" is a *social action* of an agent A towards an agent B; and the consequent social relation between them. A has some goal that he cannot achieve alone, either for lack of competences or of resources, or because it needs co-power: the coordination of the powers of multiple subjects, collective powers. We can say [9] that in delegation:

- an agent (A) needs or likes an action of another agent (B) and includes it in its own plan
- is trying to achieve some of its goals through B's actions
- thus, A has the goal that B performs a given action

Thus, A depends-on B (individual or collective), needs B's action and competence and willingness. A after the decision to delegate that goal realisation to B, will "rely" on B, "count-on" B doing what s/he has to do. If B accepts such a dependence of A on her/his, such delegation, s/he is implicitly or explicitly "committed" with A; s/he gets some *obligation* towards A about doing as expected. This form of social trust implies thus some "right" of A and some "duty" of B; and it can be "betrayed". When A trusts B, s/he not only assumes that B is able (competence, skills) and in condition to do what s/he has to do, but that s/he is well-disposed, willing, and reliable in her/his "commitment". "Delegation" is not just to pass/assign to B some *executive goal* of A's plan, some action to be just accommodated to situation and performed. We call this form *closed* delegation.

Delegation can also been *open*: that is, A assigns to B an objective to be achieved, delegating to B also to find the right plan for, to solve problems and find "how", to negotiate for possible alliances and compromises; and so on. B is not a pure executor, but a problem-solver; and A counts-on and trusts not only executive capabilities of B and her obedience, but B's autonomy, initiative, intelligence, and loyalty to values and objectives while finding the way. Of course, there is a large spectrum of openness in delegation—for a clearer picture see [8].

In our view, "open delegation" is the typical and necessary delegation in political representation; not only with vote and "representatives", but also in a party, movement, etc. More generally: to trust somebody (as decision/action not simple evaluation) means *to transfer some power of us to her/his; to give her power over us, to make us "dependent"* on her/his no longer autonomous, and accept some risk/harm from her/his side. This is well expressed in Grimen's definition of trust,[4] derived from Meyers etc.—see also [8].

On the other side, to trust somebody (or something) and thus rely-on her/it, means to *acquire new powers, to exploit its/her powers*. Trust relations and empowerment are complex and dialectic relations. For sure "representatives" should not take power from the base for them, for building their own power; but should be an instrument of empowerment of whom they represent.

2.1   Level of Help and Autonomy

In general, we can say [8] that there is a correspondent attitude to the delegation: the *adoption (help) attitude*, and in it:

- An agent (B) performs an action for a given goal, as (long as) this action (or the goal) is included in the plan of another agent (A)
- B comes to have a goal that is the same as A's, just because it knows that it is A's goal (different from simple imitation)
- B has the goal that g (wants g to be true) in order for A to achieve it

Naturally, adoption can be more or less collaborative: the adopting agent can satisfy or not the expectations of the adopted agent. In addition, the goal g can be more or less abstract and defined.

---

[4] "I shall not define them, but I shall say something about what someone who trusts, takes a risk, or *exercises power de facto* does, to show *how closely connected trust, risk, and power* are. If A trusts B, then:

1. A leaves or has something, X, in *B's custody* for a period of time.
2. *A transfers – always de facto, sometimes de iure – discretionary powers over X to B for this period of time or is in a situation where B has such powers.*
3. A values X.
4. A expects that
   (a) B is not going to do something that harms A's interests.
   (b) B is competent to take care of X according to A's interests.
   (c) B has the necessary means to take appropriate care of X.
5. A takes few precautions against B's misuse or careless use of *his discretionary powers* over X (in other words, A takes risks from this situation and he is aware of these risks.)" [14].

A real collaborative attitude of B towards the goals and needs of A, allows also that B violate the original commission or request, in order to better realise A's interest. B can do for that goal something different than expected (more than requested or some alternative way) or even bypass the required goal to realise the higher motivating objective ("over-help", "critical-help" [7]), or to care not just of current preferences of A but of A's "interests", which B might do not consider or understand for some reason (age, ignorance, moment, passions, ...) (*Tutelary* adoption and help). And A – if does really trust B's alliance – will accept such possibilities.

Political democratic "representative" relation is a relation of "open-delegation" and of "over and critical help" and "tutelary". Obviously this "autonomy" should be not in the interest or commodity of B, but for the best interest of A and in his best service.

There may be overt conflicts within such delegation and between us and our delegated: let us add something on that. A real trusted leader must have the role (and the courage) of even deciding against the current mood or opinion of the "base", since/if s/he believes that this is coherent with the value and objectives of that group/party. S/he must have such a power and responsibility: it is not an executor of orders. In case s/he is not able to convince her/his people that that was the right choice, s/he will either resign or not be reelected. Possibly, people will later be happy and convinced about the leader "unpopular" choice. This is what makes a true leader—as in the case of the decision by the leaders of the Italian Communist Party (Berlinguer and Longo) against Russia's invasion of Prague, which was very unpopular at the time among Italian workers.

The delegated is supposed to be able and in condition and delegated to understanding and deciding "better" than us, and even against our opinion or feeling, but for us, for our (group or common) good. Of course, s/he has in any case to "listen" to us, and after her/his decision to give account of that, respond, and convince (Sect. 3).

3   Transparency

Transparency is for sure an intrinsic requirement of democracy, yet not in its current deceptive popular and populistic interpretation.[5] People – against the untrustworthy "caste" (that is, "politicians") – claim full and run-time "transparency" of what "they" do and say (encouraged in that perception by the currently dominant scandalmongering press); which might strongly be facilitated by digital technology.

3.1   Dennett's Secrets About Democracy

A recent intriguing text of Daniel Dennett says [6]:

---

[5] We do not present here the fundamental and substantial reasons for which transparency has to be a pillar of democracy.

> ... understanding the subtle relationship between transparency and trust.
> And it is not what you might think—*the more transparency, the more trust.*
> *The reality is the opposite*: ...

It is true; but also because if we want to fully monitor and control the "trustee" this means that we do not trust him at all; trust intrinsically presupposes (and exploits) some ignorance about Y and some risk.

There is in fact a very interesting and not so simple relationship between trust and control. And it is exactly this relationship that defines the autonomy space of the trustee (controlled) by the trustor (controller) [10]. In our theory, we distinguish between strict and broad trustworthiness (TW), where *strict-TW* means the trustee's TW alone without special control introduced by the trustor, while *broad-TW* means the global TW of the system composed by the trustee and the additional control introduced by the trustor. In fact, we present both the cases with more control and less control with respect to a standard situation.

It is possible to show how the influence of the control (both increasing it and decreasing it) can have, in any case, an impact in both the kinds of TW (strict and broad): of course, for various different reasons. For example, an increase in monitoring and control of the political action of our representatives – with a more stringent verification of specific actions and intermediate objectives – could, on the one hand, make their behaviour more reliable by restricting the possibility of escaping from the agreed targets; but, on the other hand, it could reduce their ability to identify unplanned partial actions and objectives but apt for leading to more advanced solutions in the perspective of the shared high-level objectives.

Similarly, in the case of reduction of monitoring and control, Dennett [6] has to remark that

> We all need to keep secrets. You can't be an effective actor in the world if you expose your knowledge, plans and preferences to all people. If you reveal all your knowledge, you also reveal all your ignorance, and if you reveal all your desires, you reveal what you don't have and what you might be fearful of losing. So the vaunted ideal of complete transparency in government is a massive confusion.
> Leaders, democratic just as much as autocratic, need to keep secrets if they are going to be effective.

We do agree also on that. However, Dennett is not so clear on that, too; he prefers – for political reasons – to keep hidden (secret) some crucial part of the argument. The crucial reason of the need of secrets in democracy (and in general in politics) is not the one remarked by Dennett, but it is the fact that democracy is not just a device for collective decisions, caring about the collective good; or, just a matter of "public opinion pool", possibly well-informed.

Also in democracy – maybe it would be better say "mostly" in this political regime, where political confrontation should be the base of any deliberation – there is a continuous fight (struggle) for interests among different groups and social categories. The role of democracy is in fact to establish norms and rules through which these different and often irreconcilable interests can possibly find balance points or just prevail without social violence. The self-representation of democracy and sometimes its real attempt is to identify solutions able to overcome interests of the parts, solutions satisfying a more advanced interest for the cohesion of the various social groups.

But just because this can happen, it is often necessary, for the leading groups, to go through complex dynamic arrangements, maneuvers, alliances, attacks, and strategies; often with the difficulty of fully (or even partially) sharing these tactics with their own political representatives. And these actions cannot/should not be always uncovered (*secrets are vital*), penalty their failure! Obviously, in a healthy democracy, the conclusive results of these complex skirmishes must then be evident, public, and acceptable or criticisable for the society as a whole.

There is also another relevant reason because democracy is an advanced frontier in the guide of modern societies. Democracy has to be the tool for obtaining the "collective good", not the "good of the majority" (Subsect. 4.3). Collective and majority not necessarily coincide with each other. On the one hand, there is the need of guarantee the minority rights, on the other hand, sometimes in the minority interests there are the seeds of the better development of the whole society. So, in the rules of a democracy are in general included the rights (even if not so frequently as they should be) but about the opportunities sometimes they have to be achieved by those complex strategies that are better than being secret.

3.2 Dictatorship of Majority?

Still elaborating on the relationship between majority and minority, let us stress that democracy is not a matter of majority. Majority *per se* does neither guarantee nor define a democratic decision. Even if the 80% of people, the real "will of the demos", is for persecuting, imprisoning, expelling, etc. a 10% of the population, this is not democracy at all. A large part of despotic regimes and dictatorships enjoy a large popular consent, indeed. Yet, this does not make them democratic.

Democracy implies freedom conditions for propaganda and vote, and the protection of the right of minorities, independently from the desire of the majority. New net-democracy can help in that, both by informing, *educating* people about basic "principles" of real democracy; and by making more visible, undeniable limitation of opinions and movements, and sufferance and persecution of minorities.

But let us come back to transparency about politicians' moves, manoeuvres, and decisions.

3.3 Back to Transparency

Apart from the fact that such an emphasis on transparency is not so transparent but rather suspicious, since the (correct and important) new rhetoric of total transparency and accessibility of spending, funding, contract, relationships, investments (of governments, political parties, organizations, corporations, etc.) has as a side effect an increased public perception of malfunctions, failures and misappropriation. Suspicion and distrust increase with increasing available data, since public opinion is not so much influenced by proportion, rate (of scandals, or of crimes, for example), but by single, specific, dramatic or particularly socially unacceptable cases.[6]

There are a lot missing distinctions in that revenge, and non-accidental deviant views.

(A) First, one might very clearly distinguish between politics and administration (the real main land of corruption). Clearly, administrative rules, procedures, and actual decision and expenses should be fully transparent, public, accessible; also in the preliminary and preparatory phase (in fact, there are rules for "publicity" in tenders, in competitions for hiring, in administrative measures, and so on).

(B) Second, it is fundamental – not only in politics – to distinguish between transparency during/before a given decision and transparency downstream, post-decisional transparency.

Is transparency for surveillance of what our delegates are doing, thus for lack of trust, for reduce any autonomy in delegation? As we claimed, political job and fighting cannot work without some degree of autonomy, "open delegation" based on trust, some risk-tacking, and some secret, and even decision against the moods or opinion of the represented base (see Subsect. 1.1 and Sect. 2).

If it is true that open delegation is on the basis of the political relationships, then transparency during the activity of our representatives must be limited, partial, and give them some autonomy and secrecy. Instead, transparency *post-factum* must be total, since its function is different: is not surveillance and interference and to give "orders" to be just executed, but is for "responding" of what they have done—in order to measure the efficacy of the realised delegation and the adequacy of the representatives to that delegation.

Delegated guys, "representatives" of our powers and interests, are responsible of their actions—that is, they have to respond of them to their electors. Electors have the right and power to blame them, to ask for their resignation, to no longer vote for them and to "send them home".

If the "base" does not agree with the choice of their representatives, one has just either to persuade, win them, or to decay, to be replaced. There are non-transparent or consultation-based decisions and moves that are not real "secrets", for reasons of possible enemies etc. Politicians have to discuss and decide something without informing people just for tutorial reasons and for time reasons. They are not intentionally hidden, but not fully discussed because it is not necessary or delaying or for reasons of difficult comprehension.

---

[6] Extracted from a remark by Yurij Castefranchi, who we thank—to be found here: https://www.academia.edu/s/89deafc094/dennets-secrets-about-democracy.

What increases the level of trust in a system is not transparency—not in the sense of continuous and preliminary information about; what matters instead is the *possibility* to access to and to eventually discuss about (this can be extremely increased by information technology). Have we the power/right to (come to) know what and why you decided?

New technological powers must not be used for increasing "surveillance" and "piloting" of the representatives, but for:

- participatory debates and consultations during the preliminary phases; and
- fully transparency about what, why, by whom was decided that; and then a reasoned *evaluation* of such result and conduct.

Moreover, net-society and intelligent technology – by exploiting Big Data and social simulation – might in fact give a great contribution to real transparency, by revealing or predicting the non clear or hidden real advantages under a given law or administrative decision, the interests of which group or subject or area would be favorite. This will really be a revolution for political decision and planning [3].

However, about the request of full transparency, let us discuss another important aspect. There is another remarkable (and problematic) issue under this expectation of *radical transparency* against the need (and even the right) for secrets. Public opinion (under any political regime, even monarchy) tends to reject the idea that the "public" guys, "eminences", should enjoy the same privacy of the other private citizens; they loose this right (not from the juridical point of view but from people expectation).

Thus, *expected transparency* does not just concern the political and govern activity of the politician, but also her/his private life: private vicious are public vicious. No real distinction and separation is accepted. And, with the current scandalmongering media and gossip attitude (facilitated by web society and culture) we are close to some sort of political "voyeurism". However, it is not just a matter of envy or resentment; it is indeed a deeper problem.

The fact is that the honesty, correctness, morality of those people have public, not just private consequences: their private immorality could impact on their political morality, and in any case it can say something in general on their correctness. The fact is that we want any possible "sign" of what we can expect from them and if can "trust" in them.

This attitude challenges and stresses the general and basic distinction in Trust Theory [1] between *kripta* (hidden, unobservable) and *manifesta* (observable) features/behaviours, which is structural in trust building. We have to construct on the basis of the manifesta evaluations about one's kripta (qualities, virtues, ...), since manifesta are signs of one's internal qualities. With politicians we want to observe any observable feature or behaviour, we do not accept that something be maintained kripta (for privacy or other reasons). A politician must – also in her/his privacy – be and appear "above any suspicion": like the wife of Caesar.

4   Some of the Main Features of Democracy

4.1   Distance Represented-Representatives

A very serious problem in current crisis of democratic representation is the perceived and actual distance between people and their representatives: representatives are (or, are perceived as) far from people life, problems, feelings and motivations, and do not understand how they react and are oriented; they are not so interested or able (also for the crisis of traditional organisations of consent and movement) to listen to them or to explain to them the economic-political and governmental problems. On the other side people perceived them as caring of their own job or interests, far and indifferent to "real" problems, no longer sharing their values and objectives, etc. They do not understand and trust them.

It is very important to get closer represented and representatives, both as exchange and connection, and feeling and identity. Is web-technology an instrument for that? Yes and no. It can provide new means for that but also be deceptive and deviating.[7]

The nearness experienced (at least in Italy) some decades ago was closeness about principles, needs, perspectives, and values; and to feel close to a given class, social movement, gender, ... Not to a "multitude" of anonymous individuals, or sectorial opinion movements. Large part of these shared "identities" are now lost; it is possible to build (mainly via the web) new identities and values? The web tends to do an apparently and perceptually much greater "proximity", but it is a deceptive and deviating nearness: pseudo-"personal", perceived as direct, also on the private. "You" send to "my" address your message, your #hashtag; I react with my personal "like" or impulsive comment; I can see the photo of your pregnant partner: we are really "in touch"!

Not only this was not at all the perceived proximity with the political leaders of the time gone (like in Italian left wing Togliatti or Berlinguer), but this is not the politically needed proximity for a working democracy representing social-collective interests, not just individual contagious moods or opinions. How to improve other forms of communication, mutual understanding, listening, discussion and elaboration (like in traditional parties meetings), and shared values, identity perspectives, awareness of common social interests?

It might be that the equilibrium between represented and representative is in the "right distance" between them in their different relationships: representative has to be (and be perceived) politically close to my values, needs (interpreted as necessity of categories of people, at the extent also extremely small categories of individuals but identified by socially relevant needs/rights), to my view of interpreting society and its progress. But at the same time, the representative has to be considered as not involved in my specific and not socially relevant aspirations (then far from me). For this, a sort of distance ensures that we do

---

[7] For a good documented discussion about digital democracy, in the perspective of current post-modern democracy, of Liquid Feedback and Pirate Parties—see also Pianini & Omicini's contribution in this volume. Also relevant are their critical remarks about most common e-democracy platforms, in an engineering perspective.

not confuse friendship with political relationship. Friendship does not depend on the social value of the friend's needs. Politics must recognise the value of the citizens' needs regardless of the friendly relationships with them.

Of course, we have also to consider how much relevant is considered the "sensibility" of a politician, of her/his ability to be tuning/ in harmony/in synergy with her/his represented also solidarising on individual problematic not necessarily politically relevant. But the political action has to be always oriented only to the political nature of the relationship with the citizens.

In this sense, communication tools that intrinsically tend to confuse friendship and political relationship are instruments that deform the sense of democracy. Let us think of the interrelations that can be established between users through the most popular social media (FaceBook, Twitter, etc.). These media are very much frequented by politicians and institutional representatives, thanks in particular to their ability to spread information and opinions quickly and to a huge number of interlocutors. These media on the other hand allow you to share even very private information and establish a confidential tone between connected users.

This interactional mode naturally leads to make those relationships look like amicable and free from the restrictions that are usually suggested by more formal relationships. And this determines all the consequences we are witnessing.

In order to be a good, reliable "representative" of your interests and values and claims, X has not to be or to seem (personally and privately) "like" you, or a friend of you. Not just because s/he can be an intellectual or a bourgeois while you are a proletarian (too frequent!) but also the other way around: you are a bourgeois and s/he is just a politically very active workman or a labourer (like Giuseppe Di Vittorio, a true leader).

4.2 Conflicts: The Presupposition of Democracy

Democracy is inherently conflicting and in the same way also representation and delegation are so. Conflicts are not just horizontal (among different opinions, values, interests) but also vertical (both bottom-up and top-down):

- between institutions/government and the governed;
- between base of the same party and their delegated.

Representation has to be also conflicting to work, because there are two attitudes (delegation and adoption) (see Sect. 2) that can, at the same time, converge or diverge the one with the other. On the one hand, we have an open delegation (with a certain degree of openness), and on the other hand, we have a more or less collaborative adoption/help, with its own degree of ability and intentionality of collaboration. In practice, there is a continuous research of the optimal equilibrium between the expectation of the represented and the understanding (and ability) to perform of the representatives, in a general framework of changing needs, problems, socio-cultural-economic contexts.

No conflicts no democracy. Democracy is not only a "response" to conflicts and for moderating them; it would be a way of encouraging, growing (and solving) them. Conflicts are not just to be governed, reduced, reconciled: they should even be promoted—and this is in fact the role/function of specific forces and organisations, like trade-unions, parties, group of interests, associations, movements, etc. Crucial stakeholders of democracy, but also definitely responsible of the typical social, cultural, economic "progress" of western countries in the last centuries and now of the rest of the world.

Of course, conflicts might be dangerous conducing us to fighting, violence, wars, etc. So, it is true that societies and groups need "rules" for governing them, to avoid degeneration. Centralised state was one of these solutions: the State monopolises violence; private or group violence is forbidden.

Democracy also is a solution to conflicts; more precisely it – as we said – presupposes and needs conflicts, and would be a way of making them useful and progressive; it gives room (demonstrations, "parties", parliament, rallies, and so on) and voice and roles and rules for expressing conflicts. Not necessarily because conflicts are reconcilable, and some agreement is possible by convincing and arguing.

Conflicts are not just conflicts of views or opinion, or due to different conceptions, information, reasoning. There are conflicts of "interests": if you realise your goal I cannot realise my goal or, I lose something I have. So, the problem is conflicts between interests of groups or classes, or conflicts between "private" interests versus common interests, the "commons" and public goods.

Democracy is not just for discussion but is also rules for "winning" against the others, for changing society in favour or against some group's interests, but with shared norms and values. Social conflicts in fact do not have a "verbal/cognitive" or a "technical" solution, just based on data and technical principles; they have a "political" solution; it is a matter of "power" and of prevailing interests and compromises (equilibrium, partitions/shares).

Concluding and resuming: democracy can be conceived as the key of the peaceful and moderate resolution of conflicts. In democracy, it is possible/necessary to make conflicts explicit (on opinions, passions, values and interests), and to regulate them through defined procedures. Of course, these procedures have evolved over time based on the same evolution that have taken conflictual forms (the capacity for their identification and construction, how they are expressed, the dynamism – in the sense of strength, plurality, power, etc. – of the social bodies that support them, and so on). In practice, as conflicts and their nature change, the forms in which democracy is organised to regulate them change.

And, in a well-functioning democracy, it is the same democracy, with some forms of normation and regulation, to guide the explication of conflicts and sometimes to trigger their birth: To either accommodate or mitigate other forms of contrast/discomfort arising from dysfunctions and malfunctions in the social dynamics. It can be said that these dynamics of conflict management by democracy is the very heart of its functioning.

In a more general sense, democracy is a dynamic social artefact that changes its own structure and form on the basis of the pushing and expectations of the internal social bodies governed by it and able to be influent on these structure and form. In this sense, it can represent an advantage or a danger to the demands of freedom or equality or any other social attitude: it depends on what the direction of these pushing is. Of course, there is a limit for considering a democracy as a democracy, so the pushes cannot deform the democratic form beyond certain limits: that is, some fundamental principles/values cannot be betrayed.

4.3   Democracy and Collective Good

For sure the function of government – especially in democracy – is the collective good and defence of "commons". And a "common" is democracy itself, as political "peace", non-degeneration of conflicts, rules for social/political fighting, freedom, rights.

The *tutelage of common good* is one on the problems of direct democracy. Frequently, the best solution for a common problem is not so good locally or for some part of population. No local community would never decide that one necessary waste dump or waste-to-energy facility should stay in their area; no local community majority would decide to prohibit new building and expanding existing houses in order to protect green areas of city or landscape; no group of ten small cities would decide that the common big hospital should not stay very close to them. Of course, while tacking such (partially) unpopular decision the authority has to inform, explain, listen to, try to persuade; but not necessarily they will convince people and the decision will be locally majoritarian.

In fact, in democracy just for questions like those ones have been developed the so called "politics of compensation", in which a set of new advantages (monetary, infrastructural, practical, and so on) are offered to those populations (territory/groups) that have to undergo to specific social inconveniences or sacrifices. This is a typical example of how a problematic conflict on the collective good can be (partially) solved by the democracy evolution.

Coming back to the democracy as guarantee of the "common good", it is important to be cautious on that. It starts to be there a form of tale and ideology for justifying the limits of democracy and for disguising anti-popular decisions in the interest of dominant classes as just due to a conflict between some "common good" not understood and group/local/partial interests. Who rebels does not understand, and opposes to the common interest. But it is not always like that.

The main aim of democratic regime and of political government is managing class conflicts; where the advantages of one group (not the common good) is in conflict with the interest of another group. More realistically: actually traditional democracy has been the political expression of the power of dominant class (according to Marx: "The government is the bourgeois business committee"), yet democracy has also been a fundamental condition for organising the social and political opposition to that, for fighting against that, and achieving fundamental results.

As we said, one of the possible advantages of the new technologies is the possibility to make much more evident who is or will be advantaged by a given condition or a proposed reform. Ignorance and deception in fact still remain a basic instrument of government even in democracy.

5 Trust and Democracy

For better understanding the crucial and complex role of trust for democracy, it is also useful to realise that there are different *layers of trust*, ones grounding the others, in a dialectic relation.

As we said, it is really fundamental the trust (*A-trust*) in our representatives, since we have to delegate them to play out our power; then, electors or activists' trust in parties, associations, leaders, and so on.

However, not less essential is "trust in the system" (*B-trust*): in the democratic institutions and their working; not just in our representatives but in the oppositions, in the guarantee authorities, and – more than that – trusting that the system – with its rule and people — works, that is, is open to people needs and objectives, to base's pressures and influences. It is not self-referential, not indifferent, not impotent.

Clearly, B-trust is the ground for A-trust: if we do not longer believe in the democratic system (how it is implemented in our country or organisation) we cannot really trust our representatives and party; even if we consider them sincere and competent, we see them impotent or far from our problems or unable to change the system.

This actually is the very serious crisis of democracy in several occidental countries like Italy: lack of trust in the political system, in democratic institutions, and not just distrust in politicians.[8] In particular, the lack of B-Trust increases the abstention phenomenon (also produced by other causes). At the same time, lack of B-Trust generates also distrust, negative evaluation, in the traditional role of the politician – given the resentment and feeling of betrayal – and as a consequence an attraction towards those movements/ideas that claim a deep change of the general scheme of the political representation. In primis, "open delegation" is strongly criticised, as it considered as an arbitrary and ineffective instrument for the protection of the public good. I, as a citizen, get a hostile attitude against political institutions, representatives, parties, rules—maybe also just because I do not believe that the system can work in this way. My mistrust is then anti-party and anti-political, ready for demagogy and populist movements. I trust them but for destroying, for punishing the contempt others.[9]

---

[8] On the dramatic transformation of democracy, on "distrust", and on the need of reacting to the expropriation of democracy by hidden and strong powers, see Rosanvallon's analysis [22].

[9] On current impact of demagogy, populism, distrust, etc., in democracies, see the important contribution of Nadia Urbinati [24]. For a critical view of populism, demagogy, and their utility, see also [12] as well as the initiative of World Interdisciplinary Network for Institutional Research (WINIR) at Utrecht University on "Institutions and Open Societies" (http://winir.org/?page=past_events&side=winir_2017).

Of course, there is a dialectical feedback; not only the lack of trust in political system impacts on trust in parties and in our own referents, but vice versa: the detachment from our part and identity is not just the transition to another traditional party but maybe it is the discredit and lack of trust in the system.

6   Requirements for the Supporting Technology in Net-Democracy

(a) Voting and its freedom is a necessary but not sufficient condition for Democracy.

The vote is meaningful only if there are conditions for the formation of an informed and free judgment: for trying to change the vote of the others by changing their beliefs and preferences; to convince them, to attack and criticise the adversaries. No real possibility of large persuasion activity and impact? No democracy.

Thus, also the net technology for supporting and empowering democracy should not be focused on sending messages, photos, scandal, or in collecting opinions, trends, etc. What is needed are instruments for a real argumentation, time, attention, contradictions.

This might even increase the quality of political debate and persuasion, frequently just oriented on emotions, deception, identity, protests. In particular, these true discussion (dialogical-dialectical) instruments will be crucial in the other crucial political discussion: the debate for elaborating platforms, proposals, programs, and some level of direct decision making.

"To give voice to people" (a crucial improvement) does not consist in soliciting and receiving hashtags, reactions, consent-dissent: to test the mood of some part of the base; this is just a staging, and is very manipulable. Instead, it consists in a collective organised reasoning, building valid arguments, to learn, to inform, etc. It is not a matter of "acclaiming" a Dux.[10]

(b) Moreover, such a technological informational and dialogical support should be used for developing "critical thinking" [11,21] in people: the capability to perceive fallacies in claims and arguments, and to oppose to web "authority", to argue for a different conclusion/solution. To develop "recommender systems" not for inducing to vote for somebody (like for selling goods on the web) but for inducing better information, understanding, and possible disagreements.

(c) More than that: political fighting is not like a soccer competition where a team can have won, lost, or drawn the match, but they just try to win and the rest is failure. Political fighting is more complex: it is based on finding alliances, then on negotiation, compromise, and even with the goal of some win of some other part. Also for that – as we said – intermediation and some secret are necessary conditions and instrument for success.

---

[10] In this direction, some ICT systems seem to go in order to support discussion for decision (like in [18]—yet, this is still rather preliminary and not enough aware of political theory and problems.

(d) More than that. Net-society and communication can be exploited for involving citizens as "decentralised" and "on the field" sources, but also as "experts for experience" about the real problems of their life, and of society; and also for possible suggestions for solutions or advertising against wrong moves on that specific territory. Finally, there will be instruments (and willingness) to share these different kinds of precious knowledge between citizens (with their expertise), scientists and professional experts, administrators, and politicians, for finding the right problems/questions and the best answers and programs.[11]

As we said, however the most significant (but surely undesirable for the "establishment") contribution of the web society, Computer Science and AI systems, Big Data, smart environments, etc. would be to make "visible" (transparent!) the "invisible hand" [3]; that is, the emergent, unplanned ("spontaneous order") but non-accidental, functional, outcomes of market, political and social dynamics: who is systematically favoured by those dynamics, who is becoming more and more rich or powerful? This awareness will become really revolutionary for political movements and decisions, and democratic fighting.

We spend words on that not only because we would like to contrast the idea that there is a technical solution for the current crisis of democracy by exploiting our cyber-society, which is wrong like the idea that politics and government is a technical problem, matter of experts. Net-society can help but if exploited in the right "democratic" direction.

We are stressing those features that net-democracy should guaranty also because we believe/wish that that kind of involvement, discussion, information, proposal, decision, etc. – very different from reactive "opinions" on a social net – will bilaterally increase trust; at least trust not just as affective reaction or as faith in some guru, but reasoned trust, based on evaluations and grounded sources, and supported expectations, and thus on delegation.

Trust by the represented that feel consulted, heard by the representatives (no longer far from their real problems), but also discussed and not ignored, that give inputs, etc. They can rely on the intermediation.

Trust by the representatives that are interested in the direct experience of people involved in the concrete problems, in their willingness to propose but also hear and argument; they feel supported even in case of dissent.

And – as we claimed – trust is for us the infrastructure, the span of a working democracy that necessarily implies some level and time for delegation, autonomy, mediation and negotiation, and even secrets.

We are in favour of strongly participatory democracy (improved by the net) with some room also for decentralised and direct decisions, but against the so-called "direct" democracy replacing representative and mediating institutions.

---

[11] Take as example in that direction the pilot initiative from European community called REIsearch Program "A necessary bridge between citizens, researchers, and policy makers" (http://www.eismd.eu/reisearch/).

References

1. Bacharach, M., Gambetta, D.: Trust as type detection. In: Castelfranchi, C. (ed.) Deception, Fraud and Trust in Agent Societies. Kluwer, Dordrecht (2000). https://doi.org/10.1007/978-94-017-3614-5_1
2. Bobbio, N.: The future of democracy. Telos **61**, 3–16 (1984). http://journal.telospress.com/content/1984/61/3
3. Castelfranchi, C.: Making visible "the invisible hand". The mission of social simulation. In: Adamatti, D.F., Pereira Dimuro, G., Coelho, H. (eds.) Interdisciplinary Applications of Agent-Based Social Simulation and Modeling. IGI Global (2014). http://www.igi-global.com/chapter/making-visible-the-invisible-hand/106758
4. Castelfranchi, C., Falcone, R.: Trust Theory: A Socio-Cognitive and Computational Model. Wiley, Chichester (2010). http://doi.wiley.com/10.1002/9780470519851
5. Castelfranchi, C., Falcone, R., Marzo, F.: Trust as relational capital: its importance, evaluation, and dynamics. In: 9th International Workshop on "Trust in Agent Societies", AAMAS 2006 (2006)
6. Dennett, D.: Fake News Isn't the Greatest Threat to Democracy. Total Transparency Is. Huffington Post (2017). http://www.huffingtonpost.com/entry/fake-news-transparency-trump_us_58dd8a54e4b0e6ac7093b460
7. Falcone, R., Castelfranchi, C.: Grounding autonomy adjustement on delegation and trust theory. J. Exp. Theor. Artif. Intell. **12**(2), 149–152 (2000). http://www.tandfonline.com/doi/10.1080/095281300409801
8. Falcone, R., Castelfranchi, C.: Levels of delegation and levels of adoption as the basis for adjustable autonomy. In: Lamma, E., Mello, P. (eds.) AI*IA 1999. LNCS (LNAI), vol. 1792, pp. 273–284. Springer, Heidelberg (2000). https://doi.org/10.1007/3-540-46238-4_24
9. Falcone, R., Castelfranchi, C.: The human in the loop of a delegated agent: the theory of adjustable social autonomy. IEEE Trans. Syst. Man. Cybern. Part A: Syst. Hum. **31**(5), 406–418 (2001). Special Issue on "Socially Intelligent Agents - the Human in the Loop"
10. Falcone, R., Castelfranchi, C.: Issues of trust and control on agent autonomy. Connect. Sci. **14**(4), 249–263 (2002). http://www.tandfonline.com/doi/10.1080/0954009021000068763
11. Feldman, R.: Thinking, reasoning, and education. In: Siegel, H. (ed.) The Oxford Handbook of Philosophy of Education. Oxford University Press (2009). http://www.oxfordhandbooks.com/view/10.1093/oxfordhb/9780195312881.001.0001/oxfordhb-9780195312881-e-005
12. Fraser, N.: Against progressive neoliberalism, a new progressive populism. Dissent Magazine (2017). http://www.dissentmagazine.org/online_articles/nancy-fraser-against-progressive-neoliberalism-progressive-populism
13. Gbikpi, B.: Dalla teoria della democrazia partecipativa a quella deliberative: quali possibili continuità? Stato e Mercato 73 (2005). http://www.rivisteweb.it/doi/10.1425/19636
14. Grimen, H.: Power, trust, and risk: some reflections on an absent issue. Med. Anthropol. Q. New Ser. **23**(1), 16–33 (2009). http://onlinelibrary.wiley.com/doi/10.1111/j.1548-1387.2009.01035.x
15. Habermas, J.: Between Facts and Norms: Contributions to a Discourse Theory of Law and Democracy. The MIT Press (1996). http://mitpress.mit.edu/books/between-facts-and-norms

16. Helbing, D., Klauser, S.: How to make democracy work in the digital age. Huffington Post (2016). http://www.huffingtonpost.com/entry/how-to-make-democracy-work-in-the-digital-age_us_57a2f488e4b0456cb7e17e0f

17. Jaishankar, D.: Brexit: the first major casualty of digital democracy. Huffington Post (2016). http://www.huffingtonpost.in/dhruva-jaishankar/brexit-the-first-major-ca_b_10695964.html

18. Klein, M., Iandoli, L.: Supporting collaborative deliberation using a large-scale argumentation system. The MIT Collaboratorium. MIT Sloan Research Paper 4691–08. MIT (2008). http://ssrn.com/abstract=1099082

19. Landa, D., Meirowitz, A.: Game theory, information, and deliberative democracy. Am. J. Polit. Sci. **53**(2), 427–444 (2009). http://onlinelibrary.wiley.com/doi/10.1111/j.1540-5907.2009.00379.x

20. Lawlor, M.: The Economics of Keynes in Historical Context: An Intellectual History of the General Theory. Palgrave Macmillan (2016). http://www.palgrave.com/br/book/9780333977170

21. Mercier, H., Boudry, M., Paglieri, F., Trouche, E.: Natural-born arguers: teaching how to make the best of our reasoning abilities. Educ. Psychol. **52**(1), 1–16 (2017). http://www.tandfonline.com/doi/10.1080/00461520.2016.1207537

22. Rosanvallon, P.: Counter-Democracy. Politics in an Age of Distrust. Cambridge University Press (2008). http://www.cambridge.org/academic/subjects/politics-international-relations/political-theory/counter-democracy-politics-age-distrust

23. Urbinati, N.: Representative Democracy: Principles and Genealogy. University of Chicago Press (2008). http://press.uchicago.edu/ucp/books/book/chicago/R/bo3793416.html

24. Urbinati, N.: Democracy Disfigured: Opinion, Truth, and the People. Harvard University Press (2014). http://www.hup.harvard.edu/catalog.php?isbn=9780674725133

Democratic Process and Digital Platforms: An Engineering Perspective

Danilo Pianini[✉] and Andrea Omicini

Alma Mater Studiorum-Università di Bologna, Bologna, Italy
{danilo.pianini,andrea.omicini}@unibo.it

Abstract. The widespread adoption of digital technologies and computational devices, along with their pervasiveness in our everyday life, is going to make them hugely impact over all key processes in human societies-including the democratic one. The last decade has witnessed the emergence of many tools and platforms for *digital democracy*. However, also because of the huge social and political pressure, such emergence has possibly been too tumultuous, leaving several fundamental concerns unanswered: among them, here we focus on those that belong to the engineering process. For instance, in a classic software engineering process, one or more artefacts are produced in the analysis phase that represent a formal, possibly machine understandable, model of the domain. Instead, looking at the most common e-democracy platforms, the step is seemingly missing, along with others that concur at building a solid engineering process. This chapter elaborates on the current status of digital democracy, and points out the main software engineering issues that current and future tools and platforms should address.

Keywords: Digital democracy · Software engineering
Democratic model

1 Context and Motivation

One of the classiest and most used definitions of modern democracy comes from Joseph Schumpeter. In one of his works [30], he argues that democracy is

> that institutional arrangement for arriving at political decisions in which individuals acquire the power to decide by means of a competitive struggle for the people's vote.

Schumpeter's definition has been integrated and extended in various ways, most notably by including direct references to the *Accountability of rulers* [28]. Those definitions mostly focus on voting and competition, and do not account for several paramount issues when it comes to analysing the output of the democratic process: e.g., how political proposals are defined, who are the people who can vote, and how votes are counted.

© Springer Nature Switzerland AG 2019
P. Contucci et al. (Eds.): *The Future of Digital Democracy*, LNCS 11300, pp. 83–96, 2019.
https://doi.org/10.1007/978-3-030-05333-8_6

Nowadays, *Post-modern democracy* is a multifaceted process that is not yet deeply understood, which includes novel ways of making and amending proposals, diverse methods to express and count votes, and innovative platforms to carry out the decisional processes. In particular, the pervasive diffusion of the Internet and the Web ushered the development of novel organisational and technical platforms targeting the democratic process, paving the way towards the so-called *Digital democracy*.

In particular, LiquidFeedback [4] surged to fame, primarily thanks to its adoption by several Pirate Parties in Europe, some of which gathered a notable amount of popular support [13,17]. Whereas other similar competing platforms emerged in the last years, none of them bothered to provide any explicit *model* of the democratic process they are enacting. In all known cases, the system provides an ensemble of relevant features – relevant at least to the "common sense" version of the notion of democracy – whereas the overall precise model of democracy made available by each platform is typically left implicit, as it could be given as understood. Instead, it is well-known how diverse models of democracy exploit different decision processes, and different outcomes may result from the same initial states [9]. Also, it is unclear whether the features provided are actually required by the process to produce satisfactory results, and which is their impact across the decision making process as a whole. That sort of uncertainty potentially leads to issues: for instance, heated talks surrounded the complete Observability of votes in LiquidFeedback; and very famously a phenomenon named "dictatorship of the active ones" (also known as the "domination of the extroverts") alienated many users of the aforementioned platform.

As a result, we believe that there is a wide research space open for improving our understanding of the models underlying any novel digital democracy system, as well as of the digital platforms used to support them. In this paper, in particular, we focus on the topic of the Software engineering process behind digital democracy platforms, and try to understand how (the lack of) proper design and development techniques potentially impact(s) on the digital democracy process.

Accordingly, the remainder of this paper is structured as follows: Sect. 2 frames the current situation with regards to the main platforms for digital democracy currently available, according to a software engineering viewpoint; Sect. 3 discusses how the software engineering approaches could improve designing platforms for digital democracy, also presenting a case study; Sect. 4 draws conclusions and shapes future research directions.

2   Background

2.1   Main Platforms for Digital Democracy

In short, a Platforms for digital democracy is a software tool whose goal is letting users express their opinion and decide which option better summarises the overall idea of the community. Often, but not necessarily, such platforms also provide instruments to write and improve proposals, emend existing proposals, delegate others, and so on. We can distinguish four fundamental phases that are common to every platform for digital democracy:

1. preparation of the proposal;
2. expression of the opinion;
3. summarisation of the opinions into a decision;
4. enactment of the decision.

Many different implementations are possible for any of the aforementioned phases. For instance, the proposal preparation may range between simple proposals insertions to articulate procedures for amendment and amendment selection and application, with or without comment space. The opinion could be expressed by casting a vote, casting multiple votes, sorting the options in preferential order; it may include or not advanced features such as some kind of delegation mechanism. The extraction of the collective opinion could be performed by simple vote counting, or according to more elaborated methods, such as Borda [15], or to a specific "model of democracy" such as Condorcet [37] or others [9, 24, 29].

A change in the implementation in any of the aforementioned phases could potentially have a wide impact on the whole democratic process, influencing the involvement (both in terms of number of people participating and in terms of the social background of the participants) [20, 38], the final collective opinion, and ultimately the success of the digital democracy process.

As such, we observe that any platform defines a model of digital democracy in an *implicit* way, in spite of the fact that democracy models have been defined formally [9, 37]: although some initial efforts aimed at understanding the democracy model shaped by the platform exist [1], such a topic looks largely unexplored, yet. Instead, the requirements of awareness that comes with the promises of digital democracy mandates for the democracy model to be made instead *explicit* and *accessible* (available, understandable) to the participants, and adopted as a *first-class entity* when conceiving and implementing the platform: namely, the desired/required model of democracy should shape the platform, and not vice-versa—as it currently happens, apparently.

2.2 Basic Issues in Software Engineering

Before we dive into a presentation of the basics of software engineering, a disclaimer is needed about what is actually going to be discussed in the following. In fact, this work does not aim at summarising and comparing all the diverse approaches to software construction available in the literature and in the practice; rather, its main goal is to extract from traditional software engineering approaches those basic concepts that are relevant in the specific context of digital democracy platforms. As a result, for instance, we do not elaborate here on specific techniques such as SCRUM [31], DSDM [32], or Extreme Programming [3], and we instead refer to the more classic waterfall [26] and spiral [5] development models, as they are arguably a better fit for presenting the issues currently affecting the platforms of interest.

A (simplified) waterfall *software engineering process* is composed of a sequence of phases that lead from the idea to the implementation (where phases related to verification and maintenance are willingly omitted):

- definition of the requirements
- analysis
- architectural design
- detailed design
- implementation

When actually applied, however, the process is more similar to a spiral rather than to waterfall: quite often it is hardly possible to provide a complete analysis, or produce a flawless design, and some parts of a previous phase might as such require amendments, in which case the process gets rolled back, the change gets implemented, and the consequences propagate along the waterfall.

One interesting aspect is that each of the phases outputs one or more artefacts, possibly formal, and (as such) machine-understandable.

Definition of Requirements. The output of the definition of requirements phase is a (possibly formal) document about what is expected out of the software. It is particularly important that all the subjects involved in the definition of the requirement agree on the project terminology, as it is not unlikely that people with different backgrounds intend different meanings for the same words.

Here, the most relevant aspect concerning the definition of requirements is the separation between *functional* and *non-functional* requirements. Functional requirements are a description of the behaviour of the software should be, of its core business, and of its features. Non-functional requirements are instead further specifications that express criteria of quality. Performance constrains and security usually fall in the latter category: they are enabling requirements, but they are not strictly related to the core business of the application.

Analysis. In the analysis phase, engineers are expected to study the issues at hand, pinpointing the entities composing it as well as the relationships among them. Here it is paramount to highlight that such a phase does not account for any solution-oriented activity: before even thinking about how a problem could be solved, the problem should be studied.

The analysis phase is key, as it greatly impacts all the subsequent phases: mistakes and missing elements in this phase typically create tons of issues in any of the subsequent phases. As such, it is fundamental to invest time and resources into this preliminary phase (classic books on software engineering estimate about a third of the whole project development time). The output of the analysis phase is typically represented by a formal model of the domain.

Subsequent Phases. Once analysis is completed, the ball is entirely in the computer engineers field, who are expected to come up with a solid *software* *architecture* [8], within which the software can be designed [25], and finally tested and implemented, deployed, and maintained.

For the scope of this work, we can assume that the current practice of software engineering is advanced enough to provide effective methodologies that, when applied based on a rich analysis, produce high quality software that actually respond to the requirements [2].

3   Software Engineering for Digital Democracy

Whatever is the reader's knowledge about the basic issues of software engineering, what should be clear is that analysis plays a fundamental role in every effective software engineering process (actually, analysis is key to *any* engineering process at large): and, software devoted to enable e-democracy should be expected (at least) to provide no exception.

In particular, in our specific context of interest, the answer to our *vexata quaestio* "What is a democratic process?" should clearly emerge from the output documents of the analysis phase—or, more concretely, "Which is our model of democratic process, and what do we expect from it?". Such a generic question implies a number of other, more specific questions, such as: "Who can make new proposals?", "Who can amend them?", "How to decide wether an amendment or a proposal is acceptable?", "How does conflict resolution work?".

According to the software engineering practice, answers to those questions should not just be simple explanations: instead, they should be formal, machine-understandable documental artefacts minimising ambiguities, and leaving the smallest space possible for arbitrary human interpretation. Moreover, an important *desideratum* here is the possibility to assess up to some degree of confidence how changes to the proposed model would affect the democratic process—*de facto* producing a resilience assessment of the proposed democracy model.

3.1   A Concrete Example: Reverse Engineering an Existing e-Democracy Platform

In order to provide a reference for the reader, as well as to ground the forthcoming discussion on a concrete example, we here try to reverse-engineer an existing e-democracy platform. We extract a formal model that enables reasoning on the democratic process underlying a given platform, with the ultimate goal of better understanding how decisions are created, amended, approved and enacted in organisations relying on such a platform.

In particular, we now focus on the Rousseau electronic platform currently in use by the Italian political party "Movimento 5 Stelle" (Five Stars Movement) [33]. The reason behind such choice is twofold:

1. Rousseau is arguably much simpler than other potential candidates, such as the better known LiquidFeedback and Airesis, and as such it is easier to reverse-engineer; and

2. at the time of writing, it is in use by one of the most relevant parties [6] of a
G7 country.

For the sake of simplicity, in the following we focus on the core aspects of the
platform—namely on the subpart of the system that allows users to create political proposal and vote. Given the focus of the paper, the model we extract is
not going to take into account the following features: embedded e-learning, "call
to action" (support for event organisation), "network shield" (legal support for
members), and fund raising.

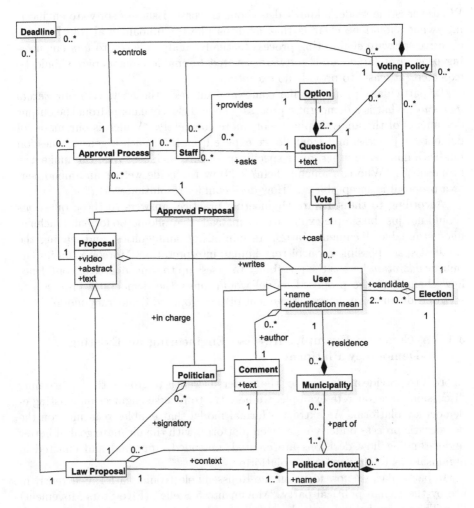

Fig. 1. Class diagram with the reverse-engineered domain model of the e-democracy
platform "Rousseau".

Formal Model Extraction: Entities and Relationships. Reverse engineering can easily get harder than designing top-down. In fact, although the object of interest already exists, it is often not design to be inspected, and it was the case with the Rousseau platform, whose documentation and source code are not publicly released. Consequently, we used the documentation and a user access to the platform to extract the domain model, which is depicted in Fig. 1.

According to our analysis, the most relevant features of Rousseau are

1. *users* can create *proposals* to be sent to their elected political *representatives*
2. representatives can present proposals to users in order to gather *feedback*
3. users can propose themselves as political *candidates*, and express *votes*
4. the *staff* can propose political questions on which the users can vote

Proposals can be freely inserted by users in the system, by providing an abstract and a text, and optionally a video explanation. Upon insertion, they are subject to an approval process managed by the staff. Usually, the evaluation process is executed in two phases: an initial filtering, and a voting procedure. In the first phase, the staff is in charge of determining whether or not the proposal is up to the standards of the community—according to the documentation, reasons why a proposal could be rejected include, for instance: the existence of a similar among those inserted in the past, a conflict with the principles of the Italian Constitution, the absence of a draft financial plan (if the proposal "looks costly"). All the proposals that get past the first phase are listed to users, which can express a number of preferences: the most voted ones get to the state of approved proposals. Once a proposal is approved, it is assigned to an elected politician, who is in charge of conveying the proposal to the proper administrative body (e.g. a parliamentary commission).

Law proposals are a way for the Movimento's politicians to get feedback from the community. It is unclear from the available documentation if such proposals get into a screening process as user proposals do. Once a proposal is inserted, users are allowed a certain time frame to add textual comments.

In case of incoming elections in a given political context (e.g. European, Italian, or regional elections), eligible users are allowed to compete in order to become candidates for the party. User eligibility is determined by residence. The staff is in charge of defining the voting policy, which includes the beginning and duration of the electoral period, and the methods to be used to cast and count votes. Neither the actual procedure nor the common routine are officially stated. However, apparently, users are usually allowed to express a number of preferences within a 8–10 hours window of a single day, and candidates with the highest preference win the chance of compete in the actual election.

Finally, the staff can propose one-time questions to the user base, providing a question, the possible answers, and a voting policy. Typical uses of such feature include decisions about the political placement and address of the party, or actions to be taken by the party leader Beppe Grillo. In the past, for instance, questions involved the choice of the group to join in the EU parliament among ALDE (liberal democrats), EFD (euro-skeptics), or none; the kind of electoral law the Movimento should push for; whether or not Grillo should meet face to face with Matteo Renzi (at the time, the incoming Prime Minister).

Discussion of the Reverse-Engineered Domain Model. Reasoning about the underlying model may help detecting unsatisfied or unexpressed requirements, or pave the way towards novel functionality. As a necessary premise for the discussion, it should be clear that the *actual* requirements for the platform are unknown; as such, it is entirely possible that the issues of the democracy model that populate the forthcoming discussion are actually a perfect implementation of such nowhere-stated requirements. A few interesting issues with the Rousseau platform that we can easily spot having Fig. 1 as a reference, are

Lack of enacting mechanisms for the user proposals —Proposals that get past the approval process are handed out to a politician for them to get presented to the proper institutional entity. However, there is no way to verify from within the system that the proposals have actually been brought to the attention of the institutions, nor to track their progress, or to link actions to increase the public awareness.

Opaque user proposal selection process – User proposals are first analysed by the staff, who may decide to refuse them. Such first moderation step is missing transparency, as no feedback is provided in order to explain the motivations behind the refusal, no complaint can be raised, nor there is a trace on the system that a proposal was actually filled in, yet it never got the voting pool.

Chaotic proposal organisation – Proposals are not categorised, they just access the competition to be selected together. It is difficult to assign priorities to proposals that fall in completely diverse and non-competing categories (how to determine what to prioritise between, for instance, children adoption policies and agricultural subsidies?).

Lack of comment moderation on law proposal – There is no (observable) moderation on the comments provided by users for a law proposal. Users may insert comments that provide no contribution, or discuss entirely unrelated topics. There is no support for categorisation or prioritisation of comments, nor a comment voting and sorting system that might help the law proponent detect what to focus upon for improving the text.

Unclear impact of comments on law proposals – There is no way to determine whether submitting the law proposal to the user base provided valuable feedback, as there is no way to link comments to amendments of the original text, nor there is a history of text modification.

Lack of transparency, observability, and self improvement – The voting policy is provided by the staff for any approval, election or question; and it is only partially disclosed. There is no way for the users to be sure their vote was correctly counted, nor is possible to intervene in the voting meta process, for e.g. proposing a different way of voting (e.g. sorting preferences in a question instead of selecting one) or counting the votes (e.g. using the Condorcet method rather than simple majority).

Centralised decision making with the questions system – The noble idea of letting the users democratically select the political placement of the party is defeated by the centralisation of the question/answer subsystem. In fact, the staff is responsible of writing both the questions and the possible answers, and might not include all the possible options. This aspect has already been a source of controversy in the past. For instance, no left-wing option was provided to voters at the moment of deciding which EU parliamentary group to join, only moderate and far-right were proposed along with a "no group" option.

This case study should clarify how the existence of a problem-modelling phase can help building e-democracy platforms that adhere to the requirements; as well as finding potential errors, shorcomings or loopholes in them.

3.2   Open Issues

As the case study in Subsect. 3.1 suggests, any existing and future digital democracy platform embodies a democracy model: however, as mentioned in Subsect. 2.1, such a model is usually implicit—namely, a product of the platform rather than the rationale behind its design. As seen in Subsect. 3.1, this may lead to serious design flaws and potential issues that may undermine the original goal of the platform.

The failure at clearly exposing the underlying model bring failures at capturing and expressing many relevant aspects of the democratic process [16]. In turn, this widens the gap between the expectations and the tool feature set, with a negative impact on usability and learning curve.

The problem is further exacerbated when the impact of an unexposed and unwanted democracy model feature comes clear: usually, the reaction is the same a software developer exhibits in front of a missing feature: a patch is released that adds the required functionality. In fact, the additional feature (or set of features), once developed without a clear idea of what is the expected result due to the gaps in the analysis phase, is at high risk of further blurring the understandability of the underlying model. The main negative impact of an unclear democracy model and a steep learning curve is the alienation of the target users [10], which may ultimately impact in a negative way on the adoption of the e-democracy platform.

The implicitness of the model of democratic process in e-democracy platforms has the doubly-unfortunate consequence of hiding the underlying democratic process, and, as a consequence, of making it extremely hard to ensure any of the required features: the richer the platform, the higher is the risk that the resulting democratic process does not correspond to the initial idea. Even worse, as there is a lack of modelling methodologies in the first place, there are currently no means to measure the distance between the implemented and hypothetical democratic process [14], and as such, for instance, to simply assess their equivalence. The icing on the cake here is the fact that those issues are nowadays hardly perceived, and platforms developers and users seems to be largely unaware of them.

Part of the problem depends on to the orthogonality of the matter: in fact, it requires understanding and expertise over an extremely diverse number of subjects, spanning from humanities to applied sciences through social and natural sciences—including, but not limited to, sociology, psychology, law, mathematics, engineering, and computer science. It is then unlikely for small teams to possess and master such a wide expertise, and – along with the typical lack of interdisciplinary cross collaborations – this makes defining/refining knowledge on democratic processes, and their formalisation as well, a difficult issue indeed.

For instance, experts of the mathematics behind voting systems tend to focus on how results differ when adopting different voting systems (e.g. sorting preferences versus casting multiple votes) or different counting systems (e.g. counting the majority, using minimax-like criteria, including information about variance, and so on). Experts in computer science may be inclined to include as many functionalities as possible in the platform, or on elaborating on issues such as security or usability; and similarly for "vertical" experts on other subjects. Democracy is however a multifaceted and cross-subject process, and cannot be reduced to any of the single views that experts in few fields can produce.

An issue that clearly arises when looking the problem from the computer science perspective is the prevalence of non-functional requirement over functional requirement. An evidence of this phenomenon is the disparity of scientific literature devoted to modelling the democratic process, and, as such, generating from functional requirements (to the best of our knowledge, just [16]), with respect to the literature addressing non-functional issues such as security (e.g. [7,12,21,23,27,34,35]). The result are often unformalised and incomplete requirements, thus hindering the analysis phase even before its beginning.

3.3   How SE Practices Could Help

Finally facing the problem of "What to do, then?", first and foremost, we advocate that there is an urgent need to reverse the relationship between the digital democracy process and its enabling software platform: currently, the latter dictates the former. As it is well-known from the general understanding of the software engineering community, we believe it should work exactly the other way around: a clear, formal model of what the desired democratic process is (meant to be) should lead to a selection of the features that the software should present in order to act as an enabler. Along this line, a further step typically required to be explored would be represented by the analysis of the spectrum of possible implementation choices: in the case that diverse options exist for the platform to implement the required process, how do they compare?

Of course, switching the priority order between model definition and platform implementation requires time and effort: if implementing a democratic platform is *per se* a non-trivial task, extracting a formal model of a democratic process and then implementing a complying platform is way more expensive in terms of time and human resources. Moreover, we reckon that (to the best of our knowledge) there is only little and very early stage research on formal modelling of democratic processes towards digital democracy platforms. This is indeed a major hurdle on the road we sketch here, as further research is required to put in practice the few recommendations listed in this work.

Another relevant aspect where the software engineering practice could be inspirational is in giving the proper relevance to the modelling aspects of the democratic process. As it stands, there is currently a strong focus on non-functional aspects of the platforms, such as security and privacy. Whereas we believe that such issues are paramount, at the same time they cannot be considered as more relevant than the issue that stands at the real core of the matter: the democratic process itself. Functional requirements should be explicit, formalised, and as complete as possible. In fact, without any formal and reproducible requirement collection, there may be ambiguities; a formalisation is key in avoiding them.

Ultimately, once the platform is deployed, continuous *monitoring* of participation, involvement, and opinion formation should be put in place: also in this regard, suitable metrics and methods (possibly model-independent) are required, with particular attention to the potential conflict among observability, security, and user privacy.

4   Conclusion

In this work we elaborate on some of the open issues for existing e-democracy platforms. We focus on comparing the existing examples with the methodologies suggested by the current practice in software engineering, and we argue that the latter could be a source of inspiration for producing better tools in future. In particular, we reckon that there is not enough attention on the functional requirements of digital democracy platforms, and that there is no formalisation of the *model of democracy* that the platforms embed. We believe that such a model should be clearly framed, and it should dictate the features of the platform—not vice-versa, as it seemingly is as of today.

There are a number of open issues in need of scientific and technical attention. There are no standard techniques for systematically acquire and organise requirements in the fields. Quality metrics and methodologies to apply them are missing, and it is hard to determine whether or not the collected requirements are satisfactorily complete. Also, it is still unclear which kind of formalism could provide a reasonable trade-off between the need of capturing the complexity of the whole process without introducing ambiguities. The development process should be systematic and reproducible, and an integral and coherent methodological approach is clearly needed [16,36].

We strongly believe that there is wide space for further research, and that such research requires a strongly-multidisciplinary effort: currently, many issues remain open, and many key questions are still unanswered. As far as one can see today, that novel body of research could exploit the literature on e-government at large as source of inspiration [11,19,22], though a focussed effort is required to tackle e-democracy, as e-government cannot be considered preparatory alone [18].

References

1. Aragón, P., Gómez, V., Kaltenbrunner, A.: Measuring platform effects in digital democracy. In: The Internet, Policy & Politics Conference (IPPC 2016) (2016). http://blogs.oii.ox.ac.uk/ipp-conference/sites/ipp/files/documents/measuring-platform-effects-in-digital-democracy.pdf
2. Aydinli, Ö.F., Brinkkemper, S., Ravesteyn, P.: Business process improvement in organizational design of e-government services. Electron. J. e-Gov. 7(2), 123–134 (2009). http://ejeg.com/volume7/issue2/p123
3. Beck, K., Andres, C.: Extreme Programming Explained: Embrace Change, 2nd (edn.) Addison-Wesley Professional (2004). http://www.pearson.com/us/higher-education/program/Beck-Extreme-Programming-Explained-Embrace-Change-2nd-Edition/PGM155384.html
4. Behrens, J., Kistner, A., Nitsche, A., Swierczek, B.: The Principles of LiquidFeedback. Interaktive Demokratie e.V. (2014). http://principles.liquidfeedback.org
5. Boehm, B.W.: A spiral model of software development and enhancement. Computer 21(5), 61–72 (1988). http://ieeexplore.ieee.org/document/59/
6. Ceccarini, L., Bordignon, F.: The five stars continue to shine: the consolidation of Grillo's 'movement party' in Italy. Contemp. Ital. Polit. 8(2), 131–159 (2016). https://doi.org/10.1080/23248823.2016.1202667
7. Choi, S.O., Kim, B.C.: Voter intention to use e-voting technologies: security, technology acceptance, election type, and political ideology. J. Inf. Technol. Polit. 9(4), 433–452 (2012). https://doi.org/10.1080/19331681.2012.710042
8. Clements, P., et al.: Documenting Software Architectures: Views and Beyond, 2nd edn. Addison-Wesley Professional (2010). http://www.pearsoned.co.uk/bookshop/detail.asp?item=100000000275802
9. Contucci, P., Panizzi, E., Ricci-Tersenghi, F., Sîrbu, A.: Egalitarianism in the rank aggregation problem: a new dimension for democracy. Qual. Quant. 50(3), 1185–1200 (2016). https://doi.org/10.1007/s11135-015-0197-x
10. Corradini, F., Falcioni, D., Polini, A., Polzonetti, A., Re, B.: Designing quality business processes for E-government digital services. In: Wimmer, M.A., Chappelet, J.-L., Janssen, M., Scholl, H.J. (eds.) EGOV 2010. LNCS, vol. 6228, pp. 424–435. Springer, Heidelberg (2010). https://doi.org/10.1007/978-3-642-14799-9_36
11. Corradini, F., Polini, A., Polzonetti, A., Re, B.: Business processes verification for E-government service delivery. Inf. Syst. Manag. 27(4), 293–308 (2010). https://doi.org/10.1080/10580530.2010.514164
12. Damgård, I., Groth, J., Salomonsen, G.: The theory and implementation of an electronic voting system. In: Gritzalis, D.A. (ed.) Secure Electronic Voting, Advances in Information Security, vol. 7, pp. 77–99. Springer, Heidelberg (2003). https://doi.org/10.1007/978-1-4615-0239-5_6
13. Erlingsson, G.Ó., Persson, M.: The Swedish pirate party and the 2009 European parliament election: protest or issue voting? Politics 31(3), 121–128 (2011). https://doi.org/10.1111/j.1467-9256.2011.01411.x
14. Francesco, A.: Benchmarking electronic democracy. In: Anttiroiko, A.V., Malkia, M. (eds.) Encyclopedia of Digital Government, chap. 20, pp. 135-140. IGI Global (2007). http://www.igi-global.com/chapter/benchmarking-electonic-democracy/11494
15. Gardner, R.: The Borda game. Public Choice 30(1), 43–50 (1977). https://doi.org/10.1007/BF01718817

16. Grönlund, Å.: E-democracy: in search of tools and methods for effective partici-
    pation. J. Multi-Criteria Decis. Anal. **12**(2–3), 93–100 (2003). https://doi.org/10.
    1002/mcda.349/
17. Jungherr, A., Jürgens, P., Schoen, H.: Why the pirate party won the German elec-
    tion of 2009 or the trouble with predictions: a response to Tumasjan, A., Sprenger,
    T.O., Sander, P.G., Welpe, I.M.: "predicting elections with Twitter: what 140 char-
    acters reveal about political sentiment". Soc. Sci. Comput. Rev. **30**(2), 229–234
    (2012)https://doi.org/10.1177/0894439311404119
18. Kardan, A.A., Sadeghiani, A.: Is E-government a way to E-democracy? A lon-
    gitudinal study of the Iranian situation. Gov. Inf. Q. **28**(4), 466–473 (2011).
    http://www.sciencedirect.com/science/article/pii/S0740624X11000578
19. Layne, K., Lee, J.: Developing fully functional E-government: a four stage
    model. Gov. Inf. Q. **18**(2), 122–136 (2001). http://www.sciencedirect.com/
    science/article/pii/S0740624X01000661
20. Montgomery, K.C.: Youth and digital democracy: intersections of practice, policy,
    and the marketplace. In: Bennett, W.L. (ed.) Civic Life Online. Learning How
    Digital Media Can Engage Youth, pp. 25–49. The MIT Press, hardcover edn.,
    January 2008
21. Moynihan, D.P.: Building secure elections: E-voting, security, and systems the-
    ory. Public Adm. Rev. **64**(5), 515–528 (2004). http://onlinelibrary.wiley.com/doi/
    10.1111/j.1540-6210.2004.00400.x/
22. Panagiotopoulos, P., Gionis, G., Psarras, J., Askounis, D.: Supporting public deci-
    sion making in policy deliberations: an ontological approach. Oper. Res. **11**(3),
    281–298 (2011). http://link.springer.com/10.1007/s12351-010-0081-3
23. Pardue, H., Landry, J.P., Yasinsac, A.: e-Voting risk assessment. Int. J. Inf. Secur.
    Priv. **5**(3), 19–35 (2011). http://www.igi-global.com/gateway/article/58980
24. Pivato, M.: Condorcet meets Bentham. J. Math. Econ. **59**, 58–65 (2015).
    http://www.sciencedirect.com/science/article/pii/S0304406815000518
25. Ralph, P., Wand, Y.: A proposal for a formal definition of the design concept. In:
    Lyytinen, K., Loucopoulos, P., Mylopoulos, J., Robinson, B. (eds.) Design Require-
    ments Engineering: A Ten-Year Perspective. LNBIP, vol. 14, pp. 103–136. Springer,
    Heidelberg (2009). https://doi.org/10.1007/978-3-540-92966-6_6
26. Royce, W.W.: Managing the development of large software systems: concepts and
    techniques. In: 9th International Conference on Software Engineering (ICSE 1987),
    pp. 328–338. IEEE Computer Society Press, Los Alamitos (1987). http://dl.acm.
    org/citation.cfm?id=41801
27. Rubin, A.D.: Security considerations for remote electronic voting. Commun. ACM
    45(12), 39–44 (2002). http://dl.acm.org/citation.cfm?doid=585599
28. Schmitter, P.C., Karl, T.L.: What democracy is... and is not. J. Democr. **2**(3),
    75–88 (1991). http://muse.jhu.edu/article/225590/
29. Schulze, M.: A new monotonic and clone-independent single-winner election
    method. Voting Matters **17**, 9–19 (2003). http://www.votingmatters.org.uk/
    issue17/i17p3.pdf
30. Schumpeter, J.A.: Capitalism, Socialism and Democracy, 1st edn. Harper & Broth-
    ers, New York City (1942)
31. Schwaber, K., Beedle, M.: Agile Software Development with Scrum, 1st
    (edn.) Prentice Hall, Upper Saddle River (2001). http://dl.acm.org/citation.cfm?
    id=559553
32. Stapleton, J.: Shop Books DSDM, Dynamic Systems Development Method: The
    Method in Practice. Addison-Wesley, Boston (1997). http://dl.acm.org/citation.
    cfm?id=523335

33. Tronconi, F. (ed.): Beppe Grillo's Five Star Movement Organisation, Communication and Ideology. Routledge (2015). http://www.routledge.com/Beppe-Grillos-Five-Star-Movement-Organisation-Communication-and-Ideology/Tronconi/p/book/9781472436634

34. Wimmer, M., Bredow, B.v.: A holistic approach for providing security solutions in e-Government. In: 35th Annual Hawaii International Conference on System Sciences (HICSS 2002), pp. 1715–1724. IEEE Computer Society (2002). http://ieeexplore.ieee.org/document/994083/

35. Xenakis, A., Macintosh, A.: Procedural security in electronic voting. In: 37th Annual Hawaii International Conference on System Sciences (HICSS 2004). IEEE, Big Island, 5–8 January 2004. http://ieeexplore.ieee.org/document/1265299/

36. Yang, L., Lan, G.Z.: Internet's impact on expert-citizen interactions in public policymaking–a meta analysis. Gov. Inf. Q. **27**(4), 431–441 (2010). http://www.sciencedirect.com/science/article/pii/S0740624X1000064X, Special Issue: Open/Transparent Government

37. Young, H.P.: Condorcet's theory of voting. Am. Polit. Sci. Rev. **82**(4), 1231–1244 (1988). http://www.jstor.org/stable/1961757

38. de Zúñiga, H.G., Veenstra, A., Vraga, E., Shah, D.: Digital democracy: reimagining pathways to political participation. J. Inf. Technol. Polit. **7**(1), 36–51 (2010). https://doi.org/10.1080/19331680903316742

Author Index

Castelfranchi, Cristiano   62
Cicognani, Elvira   1
Contucci, Pierluigi   24

Diaconescu, Ada   38

Falcone, Rino   62

Laslier, Jean-François   14

Ober, Josiah   38
Omicini, Andrea   83

Pianini, Danilo   83
Pitt, Jeremy   38

Sîrbu, Alina   24

Zani, Bruna   1

Subject Index

A

A-trust 78
accountability of rulers 83
aggregation of votes 24
Airesis 87
alienation 8
apathy 8
apolitical vs. antipolitical 4
approval voting 16
Athens 42, 55

B

B-trust 78
barriers to participation 9
Big Data 52
Bitcoin 47
blockchain 47
Bobbio, Norberto 63
Borda method 34, 85
Borda rule 16

C

CATCH-EyoU 1, 10
Cavalieri, Bonaventura 27
centrist candidate 15
civic participation 3
closed party lists 20
cognitive factors 7
collective action problem 44
collective awareness 46
collective coordination 44, 45
collective decision-making 44, 45
collective good 77
collective memory 44, 45
combinatorial structure of the voting space 28
common-pool resource management 40
Condorcet 24, 85
Condorcet paradox 26
Condorcet solution 27

Condorcet winner 16
conflict 62, 75
conflict of interests 64
consensual candidates 19
consensus 25
conventional forms of participation 3
cumulative voting 20

D

delegation 62, 67
deliberative assemblies 45, 48
demographic factors 5
Dennett, Daniel 69
desertion of the non-viable candidates 17
dichotomous vs. multivalued preference 25
dictatorship of the active ones 84
digital democracy 64, 84
distance among votes 26
distributed consensus 47, 51
domination of the extroverts 84

E

education factors 7
egalitarianism 24
emotions in civic engagement 8
ethnicity in civic engagement 5
European Parliament 20
evaluative voting 18
event calculus 50
experimental economics 14
experiments in political science 14
external efficacy 9
extreme left candidate 15
extreme right candidate 15

F

family factors 6
features of socio-technical systems 40
first-past-the-post voting 16

Fubini group   25
Fubini numbers   25
Fubini space   28
functional vs. non-functional requirements
    86

G
Gini, Corrado   28

H
Habermas, Jurgen   63
heuristic voting methods   31

I
IAD methodology   41
in-situ experiments   14, 18
institutional design principles   39
institutional structuration   46, 51
institutionalised power   42
institutions   41
invisible hand   80
iron law of oligarchy   39, 41

K
Kahneman, Daniel   29
Kemeny distance   28
Kemeny-Young method   28
knowledge aggregation   43, 45, 47
knowledge alignment   43, 46, 48
knowledge codification   43, 46, 50
knowledge commons   46, 50
knowledge management   42

L
layers of trust   78
LiquidFeedback   84, 87
living space management   40
Lull, Ramon   28

M
macro-level contextual factors   6
MACS   49
majoritarian tyranny   47
manifest vs. latent participation   4
Marx, Karl   77
McLuhan, Marshall   54

mean distance   27
media factors   7
Minecraft   50
model of democracy   85
moderate left candidate   15
moderate right candidate   15
Movimento 5 Stelle   87

N
Nash equilibrium   17
non-conventional forms of participation   3
non-participatory behaviour   4
NP-complete problems   25

O
observability of votes   84
on-line democracy   62
on-line experiments   19
opportunities for participation   9
organizational membership factors   7
Ostrom, Elinor   39, 40

P
panachage   20
Pareto frontier   37
participation rate   18
participatory vs. deliberative democracy   63
path-dependency   17
Paxos protocol   47
peer group factors   6
peer production   40
perceived control   8
personality in civic engagement   8
PIDOP   1
Pirate Parties   84
platforms for digital democracy   84
polarisation   28
political attentiveness   5
political interest   5
political knowledge   5
political participation   3
political psychology   14
political science   14
political trust   9
politics of compensation   77
polycentric governance   39, 42

population center   28
post-modern democracy   84
preferential voting   24
proximal factors   6
psychological factors   7

Q
Quaestio-it   48

R
radicalism   24
ranking   24, 25
rational behaviour   17
reliance   62
religious factors   7
remedial democracy   53
Renzi, Matteo   90
representation   62
Ripple   47
Rousseau platform   87
run-time event calculus   50

S
Schumpeter, Joseph   83
self-governing institutions   41, 42
self-governing socio-technical systems   42, 44
self-supervised health   40
sense of belonging   8
sharing economy   40
single transferable vote   16
social and collective identity   8
social capital   46, 49
social choice   45, 48
social identity theory (SIT)   8
social media   45, 47
social networking   45
social trust   9
socio-technical systems   40
software architecture   86
software engineering process   84
spontaneous order   80

standard deviation   30
standby citizens   4

T
the media is the message   54
Torricelli, Evangelista   27
tragedy of the commons   41
transparency   69
trust   63, 78
tutelage of common good   77
Tversky, Amos   29
two-round majority voting   16

U
unanticipated Consequences   54
Urbinati, Nadia   78
utilitarianism   24

V
violence   76
voter's expression   20
voter's ideology   20
voter's instrumental interest   20
voting experiments   14

W
wisdom of the crowds   51
workplace factors   7
workplace management   40
World Interdisciplinary Network
    for Institutional Research (WINIR)   78

Y
young people engagement   1
YPAR   10

Z
ZENO system   48
zero-contribution thesis   41

Printed in the United States
By Bookmasters